Hayley has written a wo٢
personal stories are inter
and relate exceptionally ٧
handles a difficult subject with grace and truth. I believe tnis
devotional will really help those struggling with forgiveness, and
I heartily endorse her book!

—**Julie Ganschow,** Author, *Seeing Depression through the
Eyes of Grace*; Director, Reigning Grace Counseling
Center, Kansas City, Missouri

In *Forgiveness: Reflecting God's Mercy*, Hayley Satrom invites us
into Christ's life-changing grace. In helping us to experience
God's grace, Hayley encourages and empowers us to give Christ's
grace to others. Though this is a brief devotional, it is packed
with theological truth applied to real life. There's no pretense in
Hayley's writing—she talks candidly and wisely about the costly
grace of forgiveness.

—**Bob Kellemen,** Author, *Gospel-Centered Marriage
Counseling: An Equipping Guide for Pastors and Counselors*

With our culture's descent into a cultivated meanness, forgiveness
has become critical. Hayley's devotional will help to deliver you
from the rising tide of touchiness that is dragging even the church
into bitterness. Let Jesus bless you through Hayley!

—**Paul Miller,** Executive Director, seeJesus.net; Author,
A Praying Life

Hayley Satrom is a gifted communicator who tackles the sensi-
tive topic of biblical forgiveness in a clear, loving, and practical
way. She begins by defining what biblical forgiveness is, then dis-
cusses the difficulty of forgiveness and God's continuing model
of forgiveness in his love for us. In my work with individuals and
couples in a church setting for over nineteen years, the topic of
forgiveness has entered into almost every situation. Hayley shares

some of her own impactful story, uses the stories of biblical characters, and shares God's Word to help others who struggle with grace, mercy, and forgiveness. This book will be a go-to resource for our counselors and those we counsel.

—**Joanne Owens,** Director of Care and Counseling,
Immanuel Bible Church, Springfield, Virginia

You begin to grasp the heart of forgiveness only when you behold the heart of the Savior revealed in the gospel. It's only in Christ that we have redemption through his blood, the forgiveness of our trespasses, according to the riches of his grace. In *Forgiveness*, Hayley Satrom helps us to marvel at this good news of free and full forgiveness and moves us toward forgiving those who have sinned against us. Hayley wisely walks alongside her readers, faithfully showing from the Scriptures what forgiveness is and how God helps us to forgive others. I was helped by this devotional, and I'm delighted to commend it to others.

—**Nick Roark,** Pastor, Franconia Baptist Church,
Alexandria; Coauthor, *Biblical Theology: How The Church Faithfully Teaches the Gospel*

FORGIVENESS

31-Day Devotionals for Life

A Series

Deepak Reju
Series Editor

Addictive Habits: Changing for Good, by David R. Dunham
After an Affair: Pursuing Restoration, by Michael Scott Gembola
Anger: Calming Your Heart, by Robert D. Jones
Anxiety: Knowing God's Peace, by Paul Tautges
Assurance: Resting in God's Salvation, by William P. Smith
Chronic Illness: Walking by Faith, by Esther Smith
Contentment: Seeing God's Goodness, by Megan Hill
Doubt: Trusting God's Promises, by Elyse Fitzpatrick
Engagement: Preparing for Marriage, by Mike McKinley
Fearing Others: Putting God First, by Zach Schlegel
Forgiveness: Reflecting God's Mercy, by Hayley Satrom
Grief: Walking with Jesus, by Bob Kellemen
Marriage Conflict: Talking as Teammates, by Steve Hoppe
Money: Seeking God's Wisdom, by Jim Newheiser
A Painful Past: Healing and Moving Forward, by Lauren Whitman
Pornography: Fighting for Purity, by Deepak Reju

FORGIVENESS

REFLECTING GOD'S MERCY

HAYLEY SATROM

P&R PUBLISHING

P.O. BOX 817 • PHILLIPSBURG • NEW JERSEY 08865-0817

Page design by Julia Myer
Typesetting by Angela Messinger

Printed in the United States of America

Library of Congress Cataloging-in-Publication Data

Names: Satrom, Hayley, author.
Title: Forgiveness : reflecting God's mercy / Hayley Satrom.
Description: Phillipsburg, New Jersey : P&R Publishing, 2020. | Series: 31-day devotionals for life | Summary: "Are you bitter? Frustrated? Seeking vengeance-or secretly pleased with an enemy's misfortune? Take 31 days to rejoice in God's forgiveness and discover how to forgive others by God's power"-- Provided by publisher.
Identifiers: LCCN 2020016170 | ISBN 9781629956251 (paperback) | ISBN 9781629956268 (epub) | ISBN 9781629956275 (mobi)
Subjects: LCSH: Forgiveness--Religious aspects--Christianity--Meditations.
Classification: LCC BV4647.F55 S38 2020 | DDC 234/.5--dc23
LC record available at https://lccn.loc.gov/2020016170

Contents

God Helps Us to Forgive

Tips for Reading This Devotional

EARLY IN OUR marriage, my wife and I lived on the top floor of a town house, in a small one-bedroom apartment. Whenever it rained, leaks in the roof would drip through the ceiling and onto our floors. I remember placing buckets in different parts of the apartment and watching the water slowly drip, one drop at a time. I put large buckets out and thought, *It'll take a while to fill them.* The water built up over time, and often I was surprised at how quickly those buckets filled up, overflowing if I didn't pay close enough attention.

Like rain filling up a bucket, this devotional will surprise you. It may not seem like much—just a few verses every day. Drip. Drip. Drip. Yet a few drops of Scripture daily can satiate your parched soul. The transformative power of God's Word will build over time and overflow into your life.

Why does a devotional like this make such a difference?

We start with Scripture. God's Word is powerful. Used by the Holy Spirit, it turns the hearts of kings, brings comfort to the lowly, and gives spiritual sight to the blind. It transforms lives and turns them upside down. We know that the Bible is God's very own words, so we read and study it to know God himself.

Our study of Scripture is practical. Theology should change how we live. It's crucial to connect the Word with your struggles. Each devotional contains a mixture of reflection questions and practical suggestions. You'll get much more from this experience if you answer the questions and do the practical exercises. Don't skip them. Do them for the sake of your own soul.

Our study of Scripture is worshipful. In this fallen world, we face trials, hurts, pains, conflict, anger, and outright messy situations.

It can be hard to forgive. It can be a struggle. Heart work is hard work. It takes heart work to move toward genuine forgiveness of wrongs, as you bear the liability and foolishness of someone else's sins and mistakes. An unwillingness to forgive can poison our heart and quickly morph into bitterness. There are exhortations to forgive in Scripture (see Matt. 6:12; Eph. 4:32) and warnings against a lack of forgiveness (see Matt. 18:21–35). So we pay close attention to John's warning: "If anyone says, 'I love God,' and hates his brother, he is a liar; for he who does not love his brother whom he has seen cannot love God whom he has not seen" (1 John 4:20). If you hate your brother and you are unwilling to forgive, it hinders your relationship with the Lord. A lack of forgiveness is a worship problem.

Does God's forgiveness of our sins make a difference? Can Christ help us to forgive? As Christians, we forgive because Christ first forgave us. That's the basis of our hope. Christ can reorient our wounded and angry hearts and help us to forgive because of the richness of his gospel. That's good news, especially if you are struggling to forgive someone you know and love.

If you find this devotional helpful (and I trust that you will!), reread it in different seasons of your life. Work through it this coming month, and then come back to it a year from now to remind yourself about our forgiveness in Christ and our need to forgive others.

This devotional is *not* meant to be a comprehensive guide to forgiveness. Good volumes are already written for that purpose. Buy them and make good use of them. You'll see several resources listed at the end of the book.

That's enough for now. Let's begin.

Deepak Reju

Introduction

HAVE YOU HEARD of Dorothy Holloway? Hers is a story of unimaginable forgiveness.

Dorothy lost her teenage son Brian in a senseless crime when he was shot by another teenager in a scuffle about a girl. For the fifteen years following Brian's death, Dorothy suffered what she called a "personal hell" of grief, so great was her anger and despair. Eventually, however, this heartbroken mother discovered God's power of forgiveness. "When God put forgiveness in my heart," she said, "... I could finally breathe."

On December 3, 2014, Dorothy wrote a letter to her son's murderer, James, who was still serving his prison sentence. Dorothy explained that God had given her the grace to forgive him. As it turns out, James had been praying for many years that God would enable Dorothy to forgive him for killing her son. "When I received that letter from her," he said, "I knew then that God had been listening to my prayers."

A most unexpected reconciliation followed. Dorothy and James write frequent letters to one another, and Dorothy regularly visits James in prison. James now refers to Dorothy as "Mama." When people ask Dorothy how this could possibly be, she shrugs her shoulders and states matter-of-factly, "I am his mother . . . in *Christ*. And he is my son . . . in Christ."[1]

Dorothy's ability to forgive her son's murderer is a reminder to us that nothing is impossible with God (see Matt. 19:26). It is a stirring example of powerful forgiveness made possible by the Spirit of God, who is alive and working in all God's children.

The Difficulty of Forgiveness

Does Dorothy's story make you wonder if you could radically forgive like she did?

Forgiveness is difficult. We say, "I forgive you," but in the next breath speak words of malice. We urge ourselves to love our wrongdoer, only to inwardly rejoice when the person suffers or to feel disappointed when they succeed. It feels easier to distance ourselves from hurtful people than to forgive them. Sometimes we are tempted to lash out or slander our offenders behind their backs. But forgive? Even if we desire to forgive, actually doing so seems impossible.

If you recognize this struggle, you are not alone. Forgiveness is one of the most common struggles I see in my work in the counseling room. No one escapes injury in relationships—not spouses, parents, children, siblings, friends, or exes. Though God made us to live in relationship with one another—and relationships are good!—the fallenness of this world taints our dealings with one another. We selfishly hurt those around us, and others selfishly hurt us too. No wonder so many folks feel *stuck* in perplexing emotions of disappointment, anger, bitterness, and even despair. We wonder *if* we should forgive, *why* we should forgive, and *how* we can forgive.

What Is Forgiveness?

According to the Bible, forgiveness is extending undeserved grace to wrongdoers, which includes absorbing their debts against us. We read in the Scriptures, "Bear with each other and forgive one another if any of you has a grievance against someone. Forgive as the Lord forgave you" (Col. 3:13 NIV). God calls Christians to the highest standard of forgiveness imaginable: *his* standard! God canceled our debt of sin against him—indeed, he paid it himself by dying in our place. He expects us to go and do likewise. As we'll see, he commands us to cancel other people's sin-debts against us just as he has canceled ours.

There are lots of ways we demand payment from other people for their sins. Instead of showing grace, we berate our wrongdoers, wish ill on them, nurse bitterness against them, withdraw from them, or keep a record of their wrongs. Yet Jesus teaches that having received immeasurable mercy from God, we have no right to withhold lesser mercy from others. Instead of berating, we are to speak the truth in love. Instead of wishing ill, we are to pray for God's will. Instead of nursing bitterness, we are to love our enemies. Instead of withdrawing, we are to move toward. Instead of keeping a record of wrongs, we are to hope in what we cannot see. Instead of *punishing* our wrongdoers, we are to *forgive* them.

Forgiveness is a high calling from the Lord; at times it feels like an impossibly high calling. Forgiveness is a part of what it means to pick up our cross and follow Jesus (see Matt. 16:24–25). There is nothing easy about that. To forgive the debts of those who sin against us requires nothing less than the miraculous Spirit of God working within us, transforming us to become more like Christ. We cannot forgive with our own strength.

Perhaps I don't need to tell you that. You picked up a devotional on forgiveness, after all. I imagine you know all too well what it means to be hurt by someone. I hope you will be encouraged to hear that you are not the only one. As a daughter, wife, and friend, I also have struggled to forgive. There have been times—even seasons—when I have felt stuck in my own anger and coldness, striving to forgive in my own strength and finding it impossible. By God's grace, I have also experienced the power of true forgiveness with *God's* strength and the unmatchable peace it brings. I have collected these Scriptures and meditations out of my own experiences, and others who struggle with forgiveness have helped me with this resource as well. I pray that our thirty-one days together will encourage your soul.

This Book

In this devotional, let's explore and meditate on God's words about forgiveness. We'll journey together with God as we apply the following gospel truths to our lives:

- God *forgives* us.
- God *shows* us what forgiveness looks like.
- God *teaches* us how to forgive.
- God *helps* us to forgive.

If you desire to fathom more of God's forgiveness in your life, this devotional is for you. If you have been seriously hurt and forgiveness seems impossible, this devotional is for you.[2] If you try to forgive but feel frustrated by how hard it is, this devotional is for you. If you struggle to move past even perceived slights or minor offenses, this devotional is for you too.

As you read, I invite you to pray for better understanding of God's forgiveness of you. Pray for an attitude of forgiveness toward your debtors that mirrors God's. Pray for wisdom about the ifs, whens, and hows of reconciliation. With the help of God's Spirit, we can forgive in ways that are humanly impossible—just like Dorothy Holloway.

GOD FORGIVES US

"The unchangeableness of the Lord's love, and the riches of his mercy, are likewise more illustrated by the multipled pardons he bestows upon his people, than if they needed no forgiveness at all."

John Newton, *The Works of the Rev. John Newton*

DAY 1

Remember the Lord's Benefits

Bless the LORD, O my soul, and forget not all his benefits, who forgives all your iniquity, who heals all your diseases, who redeems your life from the pit, who crowns you with steadfast love and mercy, who satisfies you with good so that your youth is renewed like the eagle's. (Ps. 103:2–5)

THE DEGREE TO which we rejoice in God's forgiveness of us will be the degree to which we are able to forgive others. It is difficult to forgive when we lose sight of God's amazing grace. Today let's remember *who* God is and *what* he has done for us!

Psalm 103 celebrates God's love. King David, the writer of the psalm, begins with shouts of praise: "Bless the LORD, O my soul, and all that is within me, bless his holy name! Bless the LORD, O my soul, and forget not all his benefits" (vv. 1–2). Can you feel the heart-swell of David's words as he exhorts himself ("O my soul") to praise God? He is caught up in gratitude for all that God has done.

Throughout the entire psalm, David reminds his soul of God's steadfast love. In verses 3–5, he recalls the many benefits of knowing the Lord: God forgives your sin, he heals your diseases, he redeems your life from hell, he shows you steadfast love and mercy, and he satisfies you with good so that you can have strength like an eagle. What an amazing God! Amen?

It's not surprising that David celebrates the Lord for forgiving all his sin. He is the Bible's most famous murderer and adulterer, after all. He abused his kingly authority and suffered God's painful judgment. So when David speaks of God's forgiveness, he is speaking very *personally*. God's amazing grace is a sweet balm to David's soul.

As we look at David's life story, found in 1 Samuel 16 through

1 Kings 2:11, we find that he was quintessentially human. He soared to high highs of faithfulness and plummeted to low lows of selfishness, just like you and me. David experienced God amidst his victories, and he also experienced God amidst his sins. The Lord walked alongside him—supplying courage, wisdom, seasons of discipline, and ultimately forgiveness and restoration. As David grew in his relationship with the Lord, he could not help but look back at God's love and praise him for it: "Bless the LORD, O my soul, and all that is within me!"

Can you relate to David? Have you experienced God's presence in the highs and lows of *your* life? How has God shown up for you? Has he ever supplied you with what you needed at just the right time? Forgiveness? Healing? Redemption? Steadfast love? Like David, do you need to remind yourself of God's kindness today?

If we are to grow in our ability to forgive other people, we must first remember who God is and what he has done for us. As we meditate on God's love and mercy, may we find our souls tender for the task of forgiveness.

Reflect: Can you trace the "benefits of God" in your life? If you have trouble tracing his kindness, read Psalm 103 in its entirety and reflect on his character displayed there. Pray for God to reveal more of his good character to you.

Act: Don't do this heart work on your own. As you read through this devotional, consider inviting a mature Christian friend to meet with you weekly to talk through your reflections and pray together.

DAY 2

Believe in God's Love

*But God, being rich in mercy, because of the great love with which
he loved us, even when we were dead in our trespasses, made us alive
together with Christ—by grace you have been saved. (Eph. 2:4–5)*

"I BELIEVE GOD saved me, but I imagine him doing it ... *out
of obligation.*" "I know in my head God loves me, but it's hard to
feel he could possibly love someone this messed up." "Maybe God
loves Christ, who covers me with his righteousness, but that's different from God actually loving *me personally.*" I hear such sentiments many times in the counseling room. Many Christians
believe the truth that God chose to rescue them from death. But
their joy in their salvation is dampened as they imagine Jesus giving his life with rolled eyes and a loud sigh.

I'm not surprised by these sentiments. They are colored by
how we humans "love" each other. It's easy for us to love someone who is pleasant. But love someone who hurts and betrays us?
That's not something we do naturally.

Let's not allow our *natural* selves to dictate what we believe
about our *supernatural* God. Today's verses give us a glimpse into
why and how our salvation took place. In Ephesians 2:1–3, the
apostle Paul explains that before we were rescued by God, we
were spiritually dead and deserved God's wrath. We needed his
forgiveness! We couldn't do anything to save ourselves, so we
needed a rescuer. Verse 4 starts with the most important two
words in the Bible—"But God . . ." Here we find the good news:
being *rich in mercy*, because of *his great love* for us, God made us
alive in Christ. So abundant is God's love and mercy that he rescues us from spiritual death, at great cost to himself. Praise the
Lord!

If we are Christians, it is only because God supernaturally awakened our dead hearts with spiritual life. As Paul tells us, it is "by grace you have been saved." *Grace.* That rich theological word means "undeserved favor." God shows us mercy and love not because we deserve it but because of who he is. Jesus Christ chose to die in our place because his character is overwhelmingly gracious, merciful, and loving.

The Bible gives no hint that God loves us because we have it all together. Quite the opposite—it says he loved us even while we were still sinners, dead in our trespasses. *What marvelous mercy.* On the cross, God took the punishment we deserved, not begrudgingly, not out of obligation, with no bitterness in his heart. He did it because he loves us. *What infinite love.* God is not man, and his love is not dependent upon ours. God loves us because of who he is.

Matchless *grace.* Marvelous *mercy.* Infinite *love.* This is the character of the awesome God we serve. Are you willing to accept his love for you? Receiving God's love more fully is the pathway to giving love more fully. If you wish to become a more forgiving person, start by meditating on God's love for you, which he showed by his death on the cross.

Reflect: Can you *really* believe that God loves you—*not* out of obligation or begrudgingly? If not, what is getting in your way?

Reflect: How is God's love radically different from the imperfect love in your earthly relationships?

Act: Pray that God's Spirit would enable you "to comprehend with all the saints what is the breadth and length and height and depth, and to know the love of Christ that surpasses knowledge, that you may be filled with all the fullness of God" (Eph. 3:18–19).

DAY 3

Trust God's Free Gift of Grace

For by grace you have been saved through faith. And this is not by your own doing; it is the gift of God, not a result of works, so that no one may boast. (Eph. 2:8–9)

IN 2012, I became a mother to my firstborn, Hannah Sue. Even as I write that sentence my eyes well up with tears. That's what happens when you have a mother's love in your heart!

Becoming a parent changed the way I love. While love is earned and deserved in many of my other relationships, my love for my children is a completely free gift. I can't explain it, except to say that *I love them because I love them*. I love them when they are cute, funny, and sweet, and I love them when they are whiny, difficult, and sinful. I love them . . . always. I'm not saying I always like how they're behaving; they are not perfect, and neither am I. But a deep, abiding love undergirds our relationship. That love is deeper than anything behavior can earn. It is tethered to their being as my children and to my being as their mother. It just *is*.

Our verses today remind us that just as my love is a free gift to my children, God's grace is a free gift to us, *his* children. Grace is God's unmerited favor. Out of his rich mercy and love for us, God saved us when we were dead in our sins. It is by God's grace we are saved! Our salvation, our faith, God's grace . . . all these are gifts from our heavenly Father. We need not earn them. Indeed, we *cannot* earn them. Our salvation is not by our own doing, and as a result there is no room for us to boast.

How many of us behave as if we need to work hard to achieve our salvation? Do we think we need to perform well to be loved by God? We look at God not as our loving parent, eager to extend grace, but as a taskmaster, ready to punish when we mess up.

Perhaps we see God this way because that's how we often function. I see a tendency in my own heart to love and forgive the people who deserve it . . . and only those people! Do you see this same tendency in yourself? Or perhaps you grew up in a home where grace was not eagerly extended. It is no wonder that you imagine that God functions similarly. The truth, however, is that God's grace *is* freely given; we need only to believe him that this is true.

God's grace can renew our hearts and supernaturally enable us to extend grace to others. As we accept God's free gift of grace in our lives, we discover new ability to offer unmerited love and forgiveness to others. No longer do people need to earn our favor. Even our greatest enemies are seen in a different light as we remember that God's mercy was extended to *us* while we were still his enemies.

God's grace is our free gift, given to us by our perfect, loving Father. Let's enjoy his grace and see how that impacts the way we treat others.

Reflect: Have you ever experienced a love that was unconditional and free? If you have, you know what a parent's love should be like and, even better, what our heavenly Father's love is like.

Reflect: How has God's free gift of grace changed your life? Does it affect how you treat others?

Act: Consider Julia Johnston's lovely hymn lyrics, and ask God to help you to receive his grace.

> Marvelous, infinite, matchless grace,
> Freely bestowed on all who believe.
> All who are longing to see his face,
> Will you this moment his grace receive?[1]

DAY 4

Know the Father's Compassion

*"But while he was still a long way off, his father saw him and felt
compassion, and ran and embraced him and kissed him. And the son
said to him, 'Father, I have sinned against heaven and before you. I am
no longer worthy to be called your son.' But the father said to his servants,
'Bring quickly the best robe, and put it on him, and put a ring on his
hand, and shoes on his feet. And bring the fattened calf and kill it, and
let us eat and celebrate. For this my son was dead, and is alive again; he
was lost, and is found.' And they began to celebrate." (Luke 15:20–24)*

IN JESUS'S PARABLE in Luke 15:11–24, a wayward son
demands his share of the inheritance, treating his father as if he's
already dead. The son then squanders the money in a distant land
until he hits rock bottom and crawls back to his father. While the
son is still a long way off, his father runs to him with compassion. It's extraordinary—Israelite fathers in long robes don't run
to their children, especially after they've been shamed by them.
But this father does! The son confesses his sin, and the father
responds by honoring him. He celebrates his lost son's return
with the best robe, a ring, and a party!

Jesus told this parable to a large crowd. He wanted them to
know what God is like. Like the betrayed father, God shows his
errant children surprising kindness. The Lord pursues his lost
children *even while* they are still sinners, and he rejoices to lead
them home.

I am particularly struck by the order of events here. One
might imagine that the father would not feel compassion until the
lost son confesses his sins. The son might be required to show his
repentance over the course of a year and *then* receive a party in his
honor. That's how it works with us, right? After we are wronged,

we make people work to get back into our good graces. They must earn back our favor. But no, the expected order is flipped on its head in Luke 15: the wronged father sees the son "from a long way off" and feels compassion even before the son has come near. He runs to embrace and kiss his son, and only *then* does the son offer his confession. There is no sense that the son must work his way back into the father's graces. He is forgiven and embraced immediately.

The father takes the initiative with his son even though he has been grievously wronged by him. He literally runs to his child with grace. I can't help but wonder if the father's loving initiative is what gives the son the courage to confess the hard thing: "I have sinned against heaven and before you."

God pursues us in love. He forgives us with joy. As we seek to grow in forgiveness, let's look to the example of our heavenly Father, who shows compassion to his loved ones when they don't deserve it.

Reflect: How has the Lord pursued you in love, even when you betrayed him?

Reflect: Meditate on Romans 5:8: "But God shows his love for us in that while we were still sinners, Christ died for us."

Act: Who can you show love and grace toward even before they've shown they deserve it? In love, take initiative by praying for the good of someone who has wronged or hurt you.

DAY 5

Join in God's Joy over Your Repentance

"Suppose a woman has ten silver coins and loses one. Doesn't she . . . search carefully until she finds it? And when she finds it, she calls her friends and neighbors together and says, 'Rejoice with me; I have found my lost coin.' In the same way . . . there is rejoicing in the presence of the angels of God over one sinner who repents." (Luke 15:8–10 NIV)

A COUPLE OF years ago, my beloved grandmother passed away, leaving her wedding ring to me in her will. It was a precious gift—not because of how much money it was worth but because of what it symbolized. That ring was a symbol of her love and devotion to my grandfather, and her giving it to me was a symbol of her love *for me*. One day the ring disappeared from my dresser. I have never hunted for anything as furiously as I did for that ring. Every piece of furniture was moved, every drawer emptied, every crevice investigated. But alas, I could not find it.

A year later, the ring reappeared just as inexplicably as it had disappeared! When I found it, I sank to the floor and wept. I couldn't believe that my precious treasure was found. Then I ran down the stairs and proclaimed the wonderful news to all who would listen. This included a baby, a toddler, and a kindergartner. They had no idea why this was such an enormous win, but they were happy to celebrate with me.

Do you believe that God rejoices over your being reconciled to him more than I celebrated when I found my grandmother's ring? He celebrates your repentance. He seeks you out when you are lost and rejoices when you are found.

Jesus says, "I tell you, there is rejoicing in the presence of the angels of God over one sinner who repents." In the parable of the lost coin, Jesus describes a woman much like myself, who loses something valuable to her and searches furiously for it. When she finds her lost coin, she not only personally rejoices, but she calls all those who might be able to rejoice alongside her. Jesus says this is a picture of the heavenly rejoicing of God and the angels when God's children are reconciled to him through repentance and faith.

Is this amazing? God and the angels rejoice over your repentance and your reconciliation with your heavenly Father.

What does this have to do with your desire to grow in forgiveness toward others? Everything! If you are a Christian, if you believe the gospel of Christ, then God celebrates over you: an enemy turned friend; a lost child found; a sinner reconciled. You must fathom and enjoy the celebratory, gracious, loving, and merciful Savior living in your heart if you desire to turn and become like him.

Reflect: Do you believe that God rejoices over your repentance? Why or why not? Do you delight in God's joy over *any* sinner who repents?

Act: Meditate on Luke 15:8–10. Ponder the thought of angels rejoicing over a lost sinner who repents. Imagine the celebration that erupted when you repented and believed in Christ. Pray for a heart that delights in repentance and reconciliation like God does.

GOD SHOWS US WHAT FORGIVENESS LOOKS LIKE

"Forgiveness unleashes joy. It brings peace. It washes the slate clean. It sets all the highest virtues of love in motion. In a sense, forgiveness is Christianity at its highest level."

John MacArthur, *The Freedom and Power of Forgiveness*

DAY 6

Forgiveness Is Possible

*Jesus said, "Father, forgive them, for they
know not what they do." (Luke 23:34)*

TODAY I WATCHED a husband and wife punish each other
during a counseling session. Don belittled his wife, criticizing
her with words like *always* and *never*. He ultimately attacked her
character, saying, "She only ever thinks about herself." Jennifer
responded by screaming at Don before storming out and slam-
ming the door behind her. Despite what these Christians know
of God's command to love one another, and despite my basic
communication rules for a session (which they definitely broke,
by the way), they couldn't resist the temptation to rip each other
apart. Forgiveness was not in the equation for them today.

If this is what forgiveness *doesn't* look like, what *does* it look
like? If we long to become more like God in the area of forgiveness, let's start by looking at our best example: Jesus Christ. Our
verse today reminds us that Jesus did not repay evil for evil. Beat-
en, cursed, and nailed to a cross, he experienced the very depth
of humanity's sin against him. We wouldn't expect forgiveness to
flow from Jesus's mouth in the midst of such immeasurable pain
and betrayal. Yet when he spoke, he said, "Father, forgive them,
for they know not what they do."

Amidst physical and spiritual anguish, Jesus cried out words
of forgiveness toward his wrongdoers. We see Christ's perfect nature on display when he forgives at such a moment. As we behold
his perfect love, we are reminded of how much *we* need that perfect Savior—we could have never suffered with such grace.

When the Roman soldiers hammered nails into Jesus's hands,
those were *real* nails. His pain was *real* pain. Christ sympathizes

with the challenge of exercising *real* forgiveness in the midst of *real* pain. He knows personally the great cost that must be absorbed when extending grace to those who don't deserve it.

While our pain will never exceed what Christ experienced, it is still real pain. Some of us struggle to forgive mere slights, and that is a difficult battle in its own right. Others face far more egregious wrongs to forgive. Consider my neighbor who was abused by her stepsiblings or my counselee who was beaten by a stranger and left for dead. Is forgiveness really possible for these women? Is forgiveness for such horrific wrongs not too much to ask?

Take heart—Christ can empathize with your temptation not to forgive. Yet when he was tempted, he did not sin but showed mercy. Let Christ's purest example of forgiveness give you fresh courage. The power at work in Christ on the cross is the same power at work in you today.

Reflect: Who in your life is the hardest to forgive? Do you believe that Christ sees and sympathizes with the difficulty of forgiving that person? Read Hebrews 4:15–16 and be reminded that he truly understands and offers mercy and grace to you in your time of need.

Act: Start moving toward forgiveness in your prayer life. Ask Christ for his power to show mercy to your offender. It does not need to be a neat, tidy, polite prayer. Talk honestly to God, out loud, and in your raw emotions. The Holy Spirit stands by, ready to help you in your weakness (see Rom. 8:26–27).

DAY 7

Forgiveness Is Faithful

And as they were stoning Stephen, he called out, "Lord Jesus, receive my spirit." And falling to his knees he cried out with a loud voice, "Lord, do not hold this sin against them." And when he had said this, he fell asleep. (Acts 7:59–60)

YESTERDAY WE MEDITATED on Jesus's forgiveness for his betrayers while in the throes of humanity's greatest sins against him. You may have read that entry and been encouraged by Jesus's forgiveness. But you may have easily had the opposite reaction. Perhaps you looked at Jesus's example and thought, "I'm not God! How can you ask that kind of forgiveness of me?!"

In today's passage, we read about Stephen, a mere man, who is stoned by his fellow Jews. Stephen follows Christ's example with the same spirit of immediate, sacrificial forgiveness, even as he is being pummeled to death with rocks. How could Stephen pray for his killers as they stoned him? The answer is faith.

Scripture describes Stephen as "a man full of faith and of the Holy Spirit" (Acts 6:5). The Bible defines faith as "the assurance of things hoped for, the conviction of things not seen" (Heb. 11:1). Stephen unmistakably believed in the promises of God. He preached about the unseen truths of Scripture to his accusers even as he faced sure risk to his life.

But it was not faith alone that emboldened Stephen to forgive in the midst of persecution. Even as the crowd turned against him, "he, full of the Holy Spirit, gazed into heaven and saw the glory of God, and Jesus standing at the right hand of God" (Acts 7:55). God upheld Stephen by the power of his Holy Spirit in his most trying hour. Jesus revealed himself to Stephen at the moment Stephen needed his assurance the most!

Does this encourage you? You do not face your adversaries alone. As you follow God in faith to do his will, God himself goes with you! He will be at your right hand, and his Spirit will give you everything you need in your most trying moments. Most of us will not be martyred like Stephen, but we may be called to unimaginable forgiveness. If so, we can trust the Holy Spirit to give us the courage we need to persevere in faith.

Stephen's faith empowered him to say, "Lord, do not hold this sin against them," even as his foes rushed at him with stones. Be encouraged that the same God Stephen knew is the God who knows *you*. The Lord met Stephen in his darkest hour and gave him everything he needed to be upheld in faith. God will also do this for you. As you look to Christ and pray for help, he will strengthen your faith when you try to forgive.

Reflect: Do you believe God can uphold you in faith as you forgive your offender? What do you fear you will lack in your hardest moments?

Act: Pray for God to grow you into a person "full of faith and of the Holy Spirit," just as he did Stephen. Ask God for courage that flows from a heart full of faith.

Forgiveness Is Unfair

"If I have found favor in your sight, then accept my present from my hand. For I have seen your face, which is like seeing the face of God, and you have accepted me. Please accept my blessing . . . because God has dealt graciously with me, and because I have enough." (Gen. 33:10–11)

DO YOU REMEMBER the brothers Jacob and Esau from the book of Genesis? In the end, theirs is a surprising story of forgiveness. When Jacob steals Esau's inheritance blessing from their father, Esau thirsts to kill Jacob for vengeance. After many years, they are reunited. Jacob still fears Esau, but Esau has changed. He forgives Jacob, welcomes his family, and rejoices in God's blessings to Jacob. Jacob, in turn, compares Esau's acceptance of him to "seeing the face of God." Esau's forgiveness reflects God's character to Jacob.

In his book *Good and Angry*, David Powlison writes, "Anger is all about fairness. But forgiveness is *mercifully unfair*. You choose not to give back what only seems fair, just, equitable, or reasonable."[1] Forgiveness is not about denying wrong done to us. It's about staring the wrong in the face and choosing to respond to it in a way that is "mercifully unfair." Seeing undeserved mercy in Esau's face pointed Jacob to God because God is the most mercifully unfair being of all. He does not treat his enemies as they deserve (see Ps. 103:10). Instead, "as far as the east is from the west, so far does he remove our transgressions from us" (Ps. 103:12).

You display God to others when you forgive.

I personally have experienced deep hurt that took me years to forgive. After years of counseling, healing prayer, and growth in Christ, I finally arrived at a place of genuine forgiveness. My counselor told me to write a letter to the one who had hurt me, with zero expectations for its results. The letter would declare the goodness of God in forgiving me for my own sin, thus freeing me to be able to forgive this person for his.

And so I did. I expected nothing in return, but this family member surprised me with his great enthusiasm to be forgiven. He was eager to meet with me and apologize, but he had never been sure how to broach the subject before—he'd felt forgiveness was too much to hope for. My unexpected forgiveness gave him the courage to say the hard things he had wanted to say for a long time, confessing his wrongs and asking for a new start. Once he knew unfair mercy was available to him, he jumped at the chance to right the wrongs and reconcile our relationship.

In hindsight, that story sounds familiar to me. Does it sound familiar to you too? Isn't it the unfair mercy of Christ that draws us to confess, repent, and become close with him? The fear of God may be the beginning of wisdom, but the awe of God's mercy— that is the catalyst for true repentance and reconciliation.

Reflect: Has anyone ever forgiven you in a wholly unexpected way? Can you see God's character reflected in that act? Are there ways you can point to God in the process of forgiving someone?

Act: If you are staring at the wrong done to you and not ready to forgive, take some time to meditate on God's unfair mercy toward you. Mercy begets mercy.

DAY 9

Forgiveness Is God-Trusting

But Joseph said to them, "... As for you, you meant evil against me, but God meant it for good, to bring it about that many people should be kept alive, as they are today. So do not fear; I will provide for you and your little ones." Thus he comforted them and spoke kindly to them. (Gen. 50:19–21)

TRUSTING GOD ENABLES us to forgive. Joseph is such a testament to this. His evil brothers jealously sold him into slavery and pronounced him dead. Joseph suffered years of mistreatment and false imprisonment. Yet God showed Joseph—over time—that his sovereign hand was ultimately in control. God was up to something good.

Painful as it was, Joseph's suffering was the means God used to give Joseph access to Pharaoh. His misfortunes led him to a position of power that enabled him to save the lives of countless people when famine struck. After years of injustice, Joseph could face the brothers who betrayed him and state with confidence, "You meant evil against me, but God meant it for good, to bring it about that many people should be kept alive" (v. 20). Joseph believed that God reigned over his brothers' decisions, and he eventually saw with his own eyes how God used their evil actions for good.

I wonder how Joseph wrestled with God's character along the way to trusting him. Scripture doesn't describe much about Joseph's heart during his slavery and imprisonment, but I have counseled enough people in the middle of their stories to know that we have all kinds of questions for God when we suffer. *Are you really in control? Are you really good? Are you playing a sick joke on me? Can I trust you?*

God's purposes may not have made sense to Joseph when he

was in the bottom of the pit or carted off to slavery, but in the end Joseph could testify boldly that whatever God ordains is right. He witnessed God's trustworthiness firsthand as grain was doled out to innumerable families who would have otherwise starved. Joseph's life reminds us that God's trustworthiness is not always clearly evident as we live out our difficult circumstances. Testimonies like his inspire us to believe "that for those who love God all things work together for good" (Rom. 8:28).

If anyone had a reason to hold a grudge, it was Joseph. Yet Joseph's *trust* in God produced *mercy*. Joseph did not deny the evil done by his brothers. "You meant evil against me," he said. Joseph forgave his brothers not because he minimized their wrongs, but because he trusted that God is always in control, and ultimately God is good. "Do not fear," Joseph reassured his trembling brothers. He spoke kindly to them and cared for them.

Forgiveness must be tethered to trust in the Lord. Put your faith in God even when you cannot fathom the good he is doing. God is *always* good, and that truth can free you to forgive others who are not so good.

Reflect: Do you trust God? If not, what keeps you from trusting him?

Reflect: Have you witnessed God bring about good when others intended evil? How does that impact your faith?

Act: Share with God the honest wrestlings of your heart. Do you feel angry with him? Tell him. Are you confused? Ask him what he is doing. Beg him in prayer to open your eyes to his trustworthy character in the midst of your suffering.

DAY 10

Forgiveness Is Continual

*Then Peter came up and said to him, "Lord, how often will
my brother sin against me, and I forgive him? As many as
seven times?" Jesus said to him, "I do not say to you seven
times, but seventy times seven." (Matt. 18:21–22)*

TODAY'S PASSAGE POINTS to the tireless nature of forgiveness. Peter asks Jesus what the limit is on forgiveness. How many
times does Jesus really expect Peter to forgive? Peter throws out
the number seven, as that certainly seems generous: "Should
I forgive as many as seven times?" Jesus's answer probably surprises him: "I do not say to you seven times, but seventy times
seven" (v. 22). Jesus might as well have said, "Don't keep count,
Peter! Just keep forgiving!"

If you are a follower of Christ, then Jesus's words to Peter are
also his words to you: "I do not say to you *seven* times, but *seventy
times seven*." Do you struggle with this? Consider these options:
Do you forgive or get angry? Forgive or become resentful? Forgive or despair? Forgive or distance yourself? It's so easy to give
in to our sinful nature rather than forgive. Yet Christ beckons us
to forgive because that's what it means to follow him. Again and
again. "Seventy times seven."

Wow, this is tough. So what about the wife who catches her
husband looking at pornography *again*? Christ compels her to
forgive. What about the father whose teenager lies to him *again*?
He must also forgive. What about the person of color who faces
prejudice *again* in the workplace? Even he or she must forgive.
God tells us to forgive as many times as we are wronged. It is an
act of worship (see Mark 11:25), a heart attitude before the Lord
who has generously forgiven us for our own sins.

If someone is sinning against you over and over again, the question of *reconciliation* arises. How are you supposed to engage relationally toward someone who refuses to acknowledge their sin or continues to hurt you even after acknowledging the wrong? We see in today's passage that Jesus calls us to unconditional forgiveness in our hearts. At the same time, we read in the preceding verses (vv. 15–17) that relational reconciliation may not always be fully possible, even when we forgive fully in our hearts. Christians are to strive for reconciliation (see Rom. 12:18), but since that is a two-sided process, it depends on the other person's repentance and therefore is not always possible.

When forgiveness (again!) seems too difficult, remember that Jesus didn't just teach his followers to forgive radically. He himself forgave radically. He doesn't ask you to carry a cross any heavier than his own, and he even sent his Holy Spirit to help you with the lift. So no matter how many times you must forgive, pick up your cross and follow Jesus.

Reflect: Who is Christ asking you to forgive again? Are you willing to obey him?

Act: In Luke 9:23, Jesus says, "If anyone would come after me, let him deny himself and take up his cross daily and follow me." Forgiveness is a radical way that we deny ourselves daily and follow Jesus. Pray to Jesus for help in picking up your cross.

DAY 11

Forgiveness Is Debt-Canceling

"The servant fell on his knees, imploring him, 'Have patience with me, and I will pay you everything.' And out of pity for him, the master of that servant released him and forgave him the debt." (Matt. 18:26–27)

TO SHOW WHAT forgiveness looks like, Jesus tells the parable of the selfish servant in Matthew 18:23–34. A king calls his indebted servant to settle his account. The servant owes him ten thousand talents—an incomprehensible amount in Jesus's day. The debt is so large that it is impossible for the servant to pay it back. So the king orders the servant, his wife and children, and all that he owns to be sold to make payment. On his knees, the servant begs the king for more time: "Have patience with me, and I will pay you everything" (v. 26). Of course, the servant can't really pay the king back, even with more time. The sum is too great.

The king shows pity to the servant, releases him, and forgives his debt. It is a snapshot of God's forgiveness of us in Christ. Though we owe to God a sin-debt that we could never repay, God, in his great mercy, sent his Son to die in our place for our sins. He forgave us in Christ and wiped away our sin-debt for good.

I remember vividly the first time the gravity of my sin resonated in my own heart. One lonely summer, I became discouraged enough that I opened my Bible even though I was fed up with God for allowing suffering in my life. I started to read the book of Isaiah, and I couldn't stop. The wrath of God portrayed in that book shook me to my core. Maybe for the first time in my life, I got scared about my spiritual state. I feared the debt I owed God and the punishment I deserved. I realized that, apart from Christ's sacrifice, I truly deserved to go to hell for my sin.

How relieved I felt when I read these precious words of

pardon: "But he was pierced for our transgressions, he was crushed for our iniquities; the punishment that brought us peace was on him, and by his wounds we are healed" (Isa. 53:5 NIV). Jesus died for my sins, and he died for yours as well, if you repent and put your faith in him.

God's pardon should feel precious to us, but sometimes the good news falls flat on our hearts. When God's forgiveness does not produce awe, we must ask ourselves if we are rightly estimating the gravity of our sin. After all, the gospel is an indictment of our sin before it is good news, isn't it? As Puritan Thomas Watson wrote, "Until sin be bitter, Christ will not be sweet."[1]

Do you properly estimate the awesomeness of God's forgiveness for your sins? The more familiar you are with God's mercy, the more you will dispense mercy to others.

Reflect: Do you especially feel the weight of a particular sin? Does it relieve you to know that God has canceled your greatest sin-debt through Jesus's work on the cross?

Act: Meditate on and memorize Isaiah 53:5. Take comfort that Jesus's wounds bought us peace with God.

DAY 12

Forgiveness Is Mandatory

"Then his master summoned him and said to him, 'You wicked servant! I forgave you all that debt because you pleaded with me. And should not you have had mercy on your fellow servant, as I had mercy on you?'" (Matt. 18:32–33)

YESTERDAY WE SAW a merciful king forgive his servant's astronomical debt. Can you believe that after such grace was extended to him, that same debt-forgiven servant turned around and *choked* his fellow servant for owing him a much smaller amount? When the fellow servant begs him, "Have patience with me, and I will pay you" (Matt. 18:29), this unforgiving servant refuses his plea and puts him in prison until he can pay. His selfish behavior gets reported to the merciful king, who summons the unforgiving servant and says, "I forgave you all that debt because you pleaded with me. And should not you have had mercy on your fellow servant as I had mercy on you?" (vv. 32–33). This time, the king delivers the unforgiving servant to the jailer until he can repay his own debt.

This parable shows us several things about forgiveness.

Being unwilling to forgive doesn't make sense. The fellow servant begs, "Have patience . . . I will pay you." It's an echo of what the unforgiving servant said to the king a few verses earlier. Yet rather than show the kind of mercy he himself received from the king, the unforgiving servant punishes his fellow servant. The unforgiving servant's lack of forgiveness doesn't make sense in light of the king's mercy. "Should not you have had mercy on your fellow servant as I had mercy on you?" (v. 33).

Being unwilling to forgive is unacceptable in the kingdom of God. Jesus's caution at the end of this parable warns those who are entrenched in an unwillingness to forgive. Just as the king puts the unforgiving servant in jail, "so also my heavenly Father will do to every one of you, if you do not forgive your brother from your heart" (v. 35). Forgiveness may be costly, but a lack of forgiveness is more costly still. If you are characterized by an abiding unwillingness to forgive, that could be a sign that God's forgiveness has not truly transformed your heart.

Forgiveness is costly for God. The unforgiving servant is keenly aware of what is owed to him, but there is no hint that he really fathoms what he cost the merciful king. We're like that servant, aren't we? We're more focused on the relational debts owed to us than God's forgiveness of our immense debt. It's our natural human way.

Yet the cost of God's forgiveness was much greater than anything we could pay—it was the price of his only Son's life. If he is willing to pay such a price on our behalf, can we—with God's help—extend mercy toward our wrongdoers?

Reflect: Whose debt can you cancel as you consider God's great mercy toward you?

Act: Read Matthew 18:21–35. Tell a friend or family member one thing that particularly strikes you from the passage or take a moment to jot it down in a journal.

DAY 13

Forgiveness Is Loving

Love bears all things, believes all things, hopes
all things, endures all things. (1 Cor. 13:7)

MANY OF US are familiar with 1 Corinthians 13. If we have
not read it ourselves, we have heard it read at many a wedding. It
is one of the best known passages on love. In it, the apostle Paul
exalts love as more important than any other spiritual gift or attribute. "If I have all faith, so as to remove mountains, but have not
love," he writes, "I am nothing" (v. 2).

How many newly married couples are surprised by how difficult it is to love in the way this passage describes? "Love is patient
and kind; love does not envy or boast; it is not arrogant or rude.
It does not insist on its own way; it is not irritable or resentful; it
does not rejoice at wrongdoing, but rejoices with the truth" (vv.
4–6). When I read this passage recently with a group of roommates who were in conflict, we were collectively struck by how
lovely this passage seems until you apply it to your own heart.
This is not just a collection of flowery words about a sweet concept. This is a description of what Christian love looks like, and
it is not easy!

Forgiveness is captured in verse 7: "Love bears all things, believes all things, hopes all things, endures all things." If we truly
forgive, it will be demonstrated by how we love despite sin and
difficulties in our relationships.

To *bear* and *endure* all things—what a challenge! Yet God
gives strength to persevere in a loving commitment despite
the pain that has been caused. With God's help, many believers
can *endure* a tough relational season. What does this look like?
They persevere by faith in God. They show obedience to God by

staying committed to the relationship. They continue in the day-to-day commitments because they know this is what God says is good. They go through the motions.

But to *hope* and *believe* all things—this is a completely different level, is it not? To *hope* is to be vulnerable. To hope is not solely to bear, or survive, another person's sin. To hope is to *engage* it. It is to engage the sin as well as the person. It is to join the fight against the sin. It is to partner with the loved one and *believe* that this sinner can change, by the grace of God. It is to believe the best about another, who has not always been at his or her best. It is to entrust the one we love "to him who is able to do far more abundantly than all that we ask or think" (Eph. 3:20).

To bear, endure, hope, and believe all things—this is a herculean task. It feels impossible. But remember, Scripture tells us that "God is love," and "love is from God" (1 John 4:7, 8). If you feel your lack, go to the everlasting source! We read in 1 John 4:12, "If we love one another, God abides in us and his love is perfected in us." It is our God of love who produces the fruit of love in our hearts. Turn to God, therefore, whose Spirit is alive inside you, and ask him to perfect what is lacking.

Reflect: Who do you love well? Who is it a challenge to love? Why?

Act: Consider the following questions with a wise, trusted friend: What in particular do you need to bear, endure, hope, or believe right now? How can God help you? What will it look like practically to turn to God for help?

DAY 14

Forgiveness Is Humble

[Jesus] said to [the crowd], "Let him who is without sin among you be the first to throw a stone at her." . . . But when they heard it, they went away one by one. . . . [Jesus] said to her, ". . . Has no one condemned you?" She said, "No one, Lord." And Jesus said, "Neither do I condemn you; go, and from now on sin no more." (John 8:7–11)

AS YOU READ this passage about the woman caught in adultery—with the judging crowd surrounding her to stone her—are you struck by the palpable shame captured in that moment? What shame this woman must have felt as her sin was publicly exposed before her community. The scribes and Pharisees brought her to Jesus as he was teaching "all the people" (John 8:2). Who was in that crowd? Her friends, parents, neighbors, cousins?

What does Jesus do in her moment of shame? He stands beside this woman, created in the image of God, and speaks up for her. His shocking message to the crowd is that he is on her side. He reminds the crowd of what they have forgotten: each and every one of them is a sinner too. No one can throw a stone because no one is innocent of sinning against the Lord.

Jesus saves this woman's life, but that's not all he does. He frees her from her shame. He releases her from public shame as the crowd recall their own sin and drop their stones one by one. And Jesus also frees her from shame before the Lord! "Neither do I condemn you," Christ assures her.

This is the power and goodness of God. He enters our lives and gives us freedom from our guilt and our shame.

Who do you relate to in this story? The woman or the crowd? Maybe you know deep shame like this woman experienced. Has your sin been on display, judged by others? Do you feel shame before God? God says repeatedly in his Word that he can free you from your shame as you repent of your sins and trust in Jesus. "There is therefore now no condemnation for those who are in Christ Jesus" (Rom. 8:1). Jesus stands beside you—just as he stood beside the adulterous woman. He releases you from your shame and guilt. Will you trust his grace and live faithfully as a response?

Maybe you find yourself standing with the crowd, rock in hand, ready to throw. We have no shortage of weapons at our disposal: self-righteous words, punishing distance, gossip, malice, and anger. What does it mean for us to hear the words of Christ in our lives today: "Let him who is without sin be the first to throw a stone"?

Reflect: Do you feel shame? Why? Do you believe Jesus can free you from your guilt and shame?

Reflect: Are you self-righteously shaming someone else? Who and how?

Act: Meditate on Romans 8:1 and ask God to humble your heart. Believe that there is no condemnation in Christ Jesus— for yourself or for others.

GOD TEACHES US
HOW TO FORGIVE

*"This isn't 'Let go and let God.' It's 'Let go, run hard
toward your Savior, and learn to trust God.'"*

Trillia J. Newbell, *Fear and Faith*

DAY 15

Set Your Mind on Christ

If then you have been raised with Christ, seek the things that are above,
where Christ is, seated at the right hand of God. Set your minds on
things that are above, not on things that are on earth. (Col. 3:1–2)

IT'S ONE THING to know that God commands us to forgive
others. It's another thing to learn *how* to become successful at forgiving. It's one thing to be *told,* "Bear with each other and forgive
one another if any of you has a grievance against someone. Forgive as the Lord forgave you" (Col. 3:13 NIV). It's another thing
to learn *how.*

To forgive well, you must start by lifting your eyes to Christ
in the heavens, where your help comes from. "Set your mind on
things that are above, not on things that are on earth." As human
beings, it is so easy for us to be focused on ourselves—our lives,
our troubles, our hurts, our needs. We set our minds on the things
that are on earth because they are tangible and easy to see, easy
to feel. But if you've been raised with Christ, then your world is a
whole lot bigger than this earth—and this earth is not your home.
You belong to the kingdom of God now, and you've got to seek
first that kingdom if you want to get your priorities straight for
the task of forgiveness. Who is God? What matters to him? What
should matter to you as his follower?

How do you set your mind on Christ? Make your personal relationship with Christ your top priority. Study Christ to become
more like him. Drink in his Word to be changed by him. There is
no shortcut for this. Forgiveness will be shallow and unstable if
not grounded in the Spirit of Christ ruling in our hearts.

A young woman I am meeting with, Kimberlee, is a great
example of this. She has felt stuck in her bitterness toward her

husband Tim for a very long time. He can be lazy and does not take much initiative to build up their relationship. This makes her sad, and sometimes it makes her very angry too. Tim knows his shortcomings and is working on them, but he still has a long way to go. Session after session, Kimberlee arrives frustrated by the overwhelming coldness she feels toward Tim. She knows she is supposed to bear with him and forgive him in her heart, just as God forgave her, and she even *wants* to do that. But how does she practically work this out?

Kimberlee has to begin with "forgiveness step one": set your mind on Christ. She is a strong believer who knows God and the Bible, but in her current season of life her spiritual disciplines have slipped. She is relying on spiritual highs of the past and not communing with Christ in the present. Life is busy; this can happen to any of us. But when we stop spending time with the Lord in the present—feasting on his Word and praying to him *now*—we will always veer off course. The world, our flesh, and the devil will direct our minds when we don't proactively set our minds on Christ.

Don't put the cart before the horse. If you want to forgive, start from the right starting place. Set your mind on things that are above so that your heart is ruled by Christ.

Reflect: How is your personal relationship with the Lord? Do you spend time with him? What helps you to direct your mind toward the things that are above?

Act: Spend time assessing your spiritual disciplines, and brainstorm what you'd like to change. Seek accountability to help you to implement those changes.

DAY 16

Pray

"And whenever you stand praying, forgive, if you have anything against anyone, so that your Father also who is in heaven may forgive you your trespasses." (Mark 11:25)

FORGIVENESS IS A vertical act between you and the Lord before it ever takes place horizontally with another person. It's a heart attitude that you must pursue before the Lord in prayer.

Jesus taught many things about prayer during his time on earth. Interestingly, he often taught about forgiveness in the context of prayer. For example, we see in today's passage that Jesus said, "And whenever you stand praying, forgive, if you have anything against anyone, so that your Father also who is in heaven may forgive you." What is he saying here? Whenever you go to the Lord to pray, you need to deal with any resentment that is in your heart. God commands you to forgive whatever you resent as you pray to him.

We see this again in the famous Lord's Prayer in Matthew 6:9–13. Jesus teaches his followers to pray, "Forgive us our debts, as we also have forgiven our debtors" (v. 12). There is an implicit expectation in the Lord's Prayer that if you're asking for God's forgiveness, you must be willing to forgive the debts of others. Jesus elaborates by saying, "If you forgive others their trespasses, your heavenly Father will also forgive you, but if you do not forgive others their trespasses, neither will your Father forgive your trespasses" (vv. 14–15). Jesus makes no bones about it. He commands that we forgive others when we pray. Forgiveness is a requirement, not a suggestion. You must choose to extend undeserved grace to your wrongdoers in your heart before the Lord in prayer. Jesus warns us that God forgiving your sin and restoring your fellowship with him is contingent upon your being willing to also forgive.

So, before you create a plan to confront the person who wronged you, have a conversation with God first. Tell him your hurts; cry out for his comfort. Open your heart to him and ask for his supernatural help to forgive the person you resent. Choose, in his presence, with his strength, to cancel the debt that somebody else owes you—keeping in mind that you are praying to the God who canceled your much greater debt to him.

Pray today, and pray again tomorrow. Forgiveness is not just a one-time momentary decision; it is an ongoing process. God will help you every time you seek him.

Reflect: Do you think of forgiveness as a matter of obedience? What are the consequences to your relationship with the Lord if you choose not to forgive?

Act: Before you pray about anything else today, prepare your heart by reflecting on whether you have anything against anyone. If you do, bring that problem to the Lord in prayer. He will help you to forgive.

DAY 17

Assess Your Heart

*"You hypocrite, first take the log out of your own eye, and then you will
see clearly to take the speck out of your brother's eye." (Matt. 7:5)*

WHEN WE ARE fixated on someone else's wrongs against us,
we usually don't see our own sin clearly. That's just the way it is.
Instead, we tend to compare our own rightness to the wrong-
ness of our offenders, and we find ourselves puffed up by the
comparison.

Our Savior asks, "Why do you see the speck that is in your
brother's eye, but do not notice the log that is in your own eye?"
(Matt. 7:3). He continues, "You hypocrite, first take the log out of
your own eye, and then you will see clearly to take the speck out of
your brother's eye." Perspective is everything, isn't it? Your wrongdoer's sin may appear in mammoth proportions under the microscope of your judgment. But Jesus entreats you to shift your gaze
from the microscope and notice the two-by-four of your *own* sin
right before you. Jesus uses hyperbole to show the ridiculous nature of pride that causes you to view yourself as better than others.

My friend Tiffany struggled to endure a difficult marriage.
For several years, her husband Jack watched pornography. His
pornography addiction threatened their relationship. When I
asked Tiffany what the hardest part for her was, she mentioned
how she wrestled with inward pride in response to Jack's sin. Because his sin had greater consequences for their unity than her
sin, she found herself believing she was a better person. A better
Christian. A better spouse. A better parent. A better human being
overall, really.

Tiffany struggled to forgive her husband because she compared his sin to her sin and found his to be worse. Her self-righteous

posture led her to distance herself from him and shame him with frequent barbs to remind him of his failures.

Can you relate to this? Is there a relationship in your life where you are a prideful judge with a false notion of your own self-righteousness? God never tells us to compare our sins with others'. Rather, we should take our sins and compare them with what *God* requires. That's the comparison we want to be affected by—*our* lack of holiness compared to *God's* perfection.

Tiffany knew that God's forgiveness was the greatest miracle of her life. Any righteousness she could claim was not her own; it was given to her by Christ on the cross. Turning away from her husband in *self*-righteousness, as if she was herself the righteous one, was irrational. She and her husband were *both* broken sinners in need of grace. Any comparison between them showed that they were the *same*, not different.

We all sin—every one of us! Until we humble ourselves before God by taking a hard look at our own sin, it will be difficult to lovingly assist anyone else with their sin. If you want to help to remove the "speck" of wrong from your brother or sister's heart, then you need to do a serious self-assessment first. Do not skip this step on the pathway to forgiveness.

Reflect: Is self-righteousness getting in the way of your forgiving someone in your life? Do you need to confess it to the Lord?

Act: Spend some time remembering the sin God has forgiven in your life. Praise God for his mercy in your life, and then confess whatever self-righteousness lurks in your heart.

DAY 18

Root Out Bitterness

*Let all bitterness and wrath and anger and clamor and slander be put away
from you, along with all malice. Be kind to one another, tenderhearted,
forgiving one another, as God in Christ forgave you. (Eph. 4:31–32)*

IN EPHESIANS 4, the apostle Paul exhorts us to "put away"
bitterness, wrath, anger, clamor, slander, and malice. Instead, we
are to be kind, tenderhearted, and forgiving, "as God in Christ
forgave you." Again we see this principle: do unto others as *Christ*
has done for you. If we want to forgive well as God has forgiven
well, let's be sure to assess our hearts and look for these areas of
sin to root out.

When you are hurt by someone and the memory of their offense festers in your heart, bitterness has the opportunity to take
root. *Bitterness*, or resentment, is very dangerous. It is characterized by an unforgiving spirit and a negative attitude. It is quick
to take offense and prone to hold a grudge. Cain is a well-known
biblical example of someone who held on to bitterness. Cain felt
he was treated unfairly and became consumed with bitterness toward God and his brother Abel. His bitterness manifested itself
in anger and self-pity and ultimately led Cain to curse God and
kill his brother. What a warning to us of the destructive nature of
bitterness and the urgency to root it out!

Next on the list are *wrath* and *anger*. Jesus warns us about
these when he says, "Everyone who is angry with his brother will
be liable to judgment" (Matt. 5:22). Indeed, Jesus compares anger to murder at the heart level. While anger can sometimes be
righteous in nature (see Eph. 4:26), it is much more often the
case that "the anger of man does not produce the righteousness
of God" (James 1:20). Like bitterness, we must root it out.

Clamor refers to the commotion that accompanies a fit of rage or obnoxious quarreling. *Slander* is speaking false evils about someone, and *malice* is the intent to harm someone. All these areas of sin are incompatible with Christian living, so Paul admonishes his readers to put these attitudes and behaviors to death. They are not the way of forgiveness.

But how do we root out such deeply ingrained beliefs and behaviors? Paul says we can put these sins away, but how? First, let's recognize that the Bible portrays bitterness and anger as *choices* we make, not just *feelings* we feel. This is important! As Christians, we are no longer slaves to sin, even if it feels like we are. We always have the freedom to walk by the Spirit and make better choices: love, joy, peace, patience, kindness, goodness, faithfulness, gentleness, and self-control (see Gal. 5:22–23). We must prayerfully *choose* to walk in the Spirit and to behave according to God's wisdom even when we don't *feel* like it. With God's help by the power of his Spirit, our hearts will eventually catch up to our obedient choices.

Reflect: Which of these snares do you find yourself most tempted by—bitterness, wrath, anger, clamor, slander, or malice?

Act: Confess your bitterness and anger to the Lord. Choose to walk in the Spirit, pray for help, and trust that God will grow the good fruit you long to see in your life.

DAY 19

Leave Judgment to God

There is only one lawgiver and judge, he who is able to save and to destroy. But who are you to judge your neighbor? (James 4:12)

WHEN WE SET out to forgive someone, it's important to deal with any judgment that has taken root in our hearts. We may feel we have the right to judge others for their wrongs, but as James so aptly puts it in today's verse, only God himself is holy enough to condemn a soul; we are not like him in this way. He created the law, and he alone judges those he will save or destroy. God's monopoly on judgment is a reminder to us that he is the potter and we are mere clay. We have no right to judge our neighbor, and we run the risk of trying to usurp God's authority when we do so.

One of my first counseling clients, Sylvia, was the picture of judgment. She was utterly entrenched in self-righteous condemnation of her husband, Phil. Phil had failed her financially. He had made some really unwise financial moves that created terrible debt. With great disdain, Sylvia divorced Phil and took the house and the kids with her. She felt sure she'd done the right thing to exile Phil from his home and family. "He deserved it," Sylvia would say with a scowl.

Once her divorce was finalized, Sylvia plowed full steam ahead into her new, more promising season of life. Truthfully, I worried about her. She was sure she had found her way, but I knew that she was lost. Her posture, her tone, and her heart's cry resounded with all judgment and no grace. Sylvia's abiding refusal to forgive her husband was a symptom of a much bigger, more serious problem: Sylvia didn't understand God's grace for herself.

Five years after our counseling ended, I received a devastating message from Phil. Sylvia had taken her own life. The house, the kids, the money she'd made . . . it all returned to Phil. It was an ironic and tragic end to a life that could have gone so differently. Sylvia's judgment did not have to consume her. What would her life have looked like if she'd rooted out her judgment and pursued humility before the Lord? Who might she have become if she'd been willing to hope in the Lord's goodness and control during her suffering?

Once God forgives our sins and welcomes us into his family, our hearts should experience an astounding shift. We transform from *trying to be* God to *worshipping* God. And amidst that massive heart transformation, we mature from *judging* others to *loving* them. Loving people can be really painful sometimes. Forgiving is costly. But we see here that judging is more costly still.

"God opposes the proud but gives grace to the humble" (James 4:6). Do not pit yourself against the almighty God. *Humility* is the key to repentance. If there is judgment rooted deep within you, turn to God, confess your sin, and draw near to him. He promises that when you draw near to him, he will draw near to you. "Humble yourselves before the Lord, and he will exalt you" (James 4:10).

Reflect: Who are you tempted to judge or condemn? According to today's verse, why should you forgive them instead?

Act: Make a list of things God has forgiven you for thus far in life—big things, small things, whatever comes to mind. Thank God for his forgiveness, and carry the humility of that exercise into a relationship where you are tempted to judge and condemn.

DAY 20

Consider Overlooking First

*Above all, keep loving one another earnestly, since
love covers a multitude of sins. (1 Peter 4:8)*

THE APOSTLE PETER instructs us to "love one another earnestly." What does that mean? Other translations of this verse
say "love each other deeply" (NIV), "keep fervent in your love
for one another" (NASB), "have fervent charity among yourselves" (KJV), and "love each other as if your life depended on
it" (MSG). "Loving one another earnestly" connotes a deep, fervent, charitable love—strong enough to cover a multitude of sins.
Peter believes that where love abounds richly, wrongdoing can be
more easily absorbed and moved beyond.

Has anyone in your life ever shown you that kind of earnest
love—a love deep enough to overlook your multitude of sins?
When I think of this kind of earnest love, I picture my grandparents. My grandparents' love covered all my flaws, and to be near
them was to bask in grace and charity. I wonder if anyone could
say the same of you or me? Do we love anyone earnestly like that?
God wants us to love earnestly, because genuine love can overlook many offenses.

Proverbs 19:11 says, "Good sense makes one slow to anger,
and it is his glory to overlook an offense." To overlook an offense
is a legitimate and biblical form of forgiveness. Scripture teaches
that in many cases forgiveness can be unilateral and unconditional in your heart before the Lord. It is possible to choose to
overlook—to suffer wrong and forgive—without being asked
and without formally confronting the wrongdoer.

Petty or unintentional offenses are the most obvious ones to
forgive in this way. When I got married, my father-in-law spoke

to this. He encouraged my husband and me "not to sweat the small stuff" in marriage. I'm really amazed by how often his advice comes to mind. It's some of the best marital advice I've been given, as so much marital sin falls into the category of small stuff. Assuming you have done the difficult heart work of forgiveness with the Lord, consider whether confrontation with your offender is really necessary.

Sometimes confrontation *is* good. For instance, it's good to confront a sin that is doing lasting damage to your relationship, because in that case confrontation can lead to restoring the relationship from the damage that's been done. It's also important to confront offenses that do serious harm to another person, to the offender, or to God's reputation. In these cases, confrontation protects someone, and it might even lead an offender to repent and change. Confrontation can be good, but it's also good to consider whether you can fully forgive without it.

Be thoughtful. Overlook sin when it's possible and confront sin when it's necessary. Either way, let your motivation be earnest love.

Reflect: Who have you felt earnestly loved by? Can you think of instances where someone's love for you enabled them to overlook your sins? Do you love anyone earnestly?

Act: This week when someone offends you, wait a day or two before responding to that offense. As I have been known to say to myself, "when in doubt, shut your mouth." Contemplate with the Lord whether the offense really warrants confrontation, or whether you might be able to suffer wrong, forgive, and move on without it.

DAY 21

Confront

*"If your brother sins against you, go and tell him his
fault, between you and him alone. If he listens to you,
you have gained your brother." (Matt. 18:15)*

THINK OF FORGIVENESS as having both a vertical and horizontal dimension. God mostly speaks to the *vertical* dimension of forgiveness—that is, our heart attitude of unconditional forgiveness before the Lord (see Mark 11:25), and so we have spent the majority of our time in this devotional addressing the heart.

As in today's passage, God also speaks of a *horizontal* transaction of forgiveness that may occur between you and your offender. In our culture, a more precise term for this transaction of forgiveness is *reconciliation*. Reconciliation involves confrontation with the hope of relational restoration, though that is not always possible.

Once you do the difficult heart work of forgiveness with the Lord (set your mind on Christ, pray, assess your own heart, and root out bitterness and judgment), consider whether confrontation with your offender is necessary. Here are two rules of thumb: (1) it's good to confront an offense that is doing lasting damage to your relationship, and (2) it's also good to confront offenses that do serious damage to you, the offender, someone else, or God's reputation. If you're not sure whether confrontation is needed in your situation, seek counsel from other wise, trustworthy Christians (see Prov. 18:1).

Assuming confrontation is the right next step, God lays out what the process should look like in Matthew 18, starting with the simple instruction, "If your brother sins against you, go and tell him his fault, between you and him alone. If he listens to you,

you have gained your brother." Start there, and have the hard conversation! Start privately, so as to initially protect your offender's reputation, and confront them with the ultimate purpose of "gaining" them to the Lord. The goal is not only your offender's unity with you, but—more importantly—his unity with God.

Plan what you want to say, and try to say it in a way that builds up and doesn't tear down (see Eph. 4:29). Demonstrate love and humility by speaking with patience and gentleness. Heed the words of Proverbs 12:18: "Rash words are like sword thrusts, but the tongue of the wise brings healing." Tell your offender their fault in a careful way.

If you expect the conversation to be volatile due to the grievous nature of the offense or the unpredictable nature of the offender, it might be best to keep your confrontation in writing at first (and maybe always). Writing requires more careful thought than speech and is more controllable than an in-person interaction. Keeping words in writing can provide a helpful buffer.

What about if your offender is dangerous? How does a victim of abuse, for instance, confront their abuser? In such cases, your priority must be to *stay safe*. Include a trusted, safe third party in the interaction, or have someone confront your abuser on your behalf without you present. Do not put yourself in unnecessary danger for the sake of confrontation.

Reflect: Do you need to confront someone who has wronged you? How can you tell?

Act: If or when you need to confront someone about their sin, seek counsel about the content of your confrontation as well as the manner. Get some advice about whether your planned words show humility and a desire for unity.

DAY 22

Be Patient

"If your brother sins, rebuke him, and if he repents, forgive him, and if he sins against you seven times in the day, and turns to you seven times, saying, 'I repent,' you must forgive him." (Luke 17:3–4)

CAMERON HAD BEEN living with resentment for years. His adoptive parents never seemed to understand him—first as a child and now as an adult. He was emotional and direct, and his parents were stoic and steady. They would often criticize the *way* in which he told them something instead of acknowledging the content of what he was saying. They would dismiss him as "dramatic" or "acting like a diva" and then fail to respond to the concern he had tried to bring to their attention.

Cameron worked hard in counseling to forgive them. But Cameron's parents needed to understand how they were hurting him if they were ever going to stop, so I encouraged Cameron to invite them into counseling with him. He prepared carefully for the confrontation—he was thoughtful about the words he used and how he used them—and by God's grace it was a very successful conversation. Cameron's parents recognized the ways they had been prone to put him down for his personality differences. When they apologized, Cameron forgave them on the spot.

This is always what we hope for in a confrontation, isn't it? We confront someone for sin, they acknowledge the sin and apologize for it, and we forgive them. It's as simple as that! Jesus taught about this. He said, "If your brother sins, rebuke him, and if he repents, forgive him, and if he sins against you seven times in the day, and turns to you seven times, saying, 'I repent,' you must forgive him." Here he gives us a picture of what relational reconciliation looks like. It includes confrontation, acknowledgment, repentance, and restoration. Notice how Jesus throws in the fact that this sin may happen again, maybe even many times again. Even so, he tells us to keep forgiving.

We wish sins would clear up immediately after a good confrontation. Sin is messy, though. Repentance is a difficult process, just like forgiveness is a difficult process. Each time you are hurt by someone's repeat offense against you, run to God with your anger and sadness. He sees, he knows, and he is the one who can truly help. It is God's power that can give you the supernatural strength to forgive, and what's more, it is God's power that can give your offender the supernatural strength to repent.

Reflect: Are someone's repeat offenses dragging you down? What do you need in order to patiently endure?

Act: Practice gratitude today, even for the repeat offender in your life—the one trying to repent but having trouble doing so. Their recurring sin is not the only thing that's true about them. In what ways do you see God's grace at work in their life? Can you tell them about it? Let that exercise of gratitude encourage both your hearts because you both probably need it.

DAY 23

Love Your Enemy

"But love your enemies, and do good, and lend,
expecting nothing in return, and your reward will be
great, and you will be sons of the Most High, for he is
kind to the ungrateful and the evil. Be merciful, even
as your Father is merciful." (Luke 6:35–36)

WE'VE SPENT THE last couple days thinking through confronting our wrongdoers and forgiving them when they repent. But what do we do when an offender *won't* repent?

If you confront your offender and they are unwilling to admit fault or change, it will inevitably affect the nature of your relationship. God still commands you to forgive unconditionally in your heart, but your forgiveness will have to be one-sided because it will not be reciprocated with mutual understanding.[1]

Jesus speaks to this dilemma when he says, "Love your enemies, do good to those who hate you, bless those who curse you, pray for those who abuse you" (Luke 6:27–28) and "Love your enemies, and do good, and lend, expecting nothing in return, and your reward will be great." Even if we have not been offended so grievously that we could label our wrongdoer an enemy, the principle remains the same: we are to persevere in love, even with the unrepentant.[2] "If you love those who love you," asks Jesus, "what benefit is that to you? For even sinners love those who love them. And if you do good to those who do good to you, what benefit is that to you? For even sinners do the same" (Luke 6:32–33). Reciprocating love is insufficient in the Christian life. Jesus challenges us to love our *enemies*. Now that is a radical request.

Believers demonstrate that they are "sons of the Most High" when they love their enemies, because God himself is "kind to the ungrateful and the evil." We show off God's mercy when we show mercy to our enemies.

Janice, a divorced woman I once counseled, was healing from a difficult marriage. Her stories of mistreatment were heartbreaking. Yet despite the betrayal and belittlement Janice had experienced, she prayed for God to show mercy to her ex-husband. I wasn't the only one struck by this. Her daughter Patrice watched her mom pray for her dad's good—year after year—despite the pain he'd caused. Patrice knew her mom's faith was the reason she persevered in prayer for her dad, and that kind of mercy was so different from what the world had to offer. The striking nature of her mom's love for an enemy attracted Patrice to God. With time, Patrice gave her life to Christ, praise God!

You never know how God may use your obedience. God used Janice's faithfulness to reflect his trustworthy and good character to her daughter. You may not expect the ways he can use *your* godly decisions and attitude toward an enemy to affect a watching world. "Be merciful, even as your Father is merciful."

Reflect: In what ways have you seen God be kind to the ungrateful and evil? Can you think of biblical or personal examples of God's mercy?

Reflect: What would happen if you showed mercy to the ungrateful or evil?

Act: Think of someone in your life who is mean, obnoxious, or even evil to you. That person is difficult to love, to say the least. Pray for that person right now. If appropriate, talk to a wise Christian friend and brainstorm a way to intentionally do good to your enemy.

DAY 24

Leave Vengeance to the Lord

Beloved, never avenge yourselves, but leave it to the wrath of God. . . .
"If your enemy is hungry, feed him; if he is thirsty, give him something to
drink; for by so doing you will heap burning coals on his head." Do not
be overcome by evil, but overcome evil with good. (Rom. 12:19–21)

LAUREN DIDN'T KNOW where to begin with forgiveness. She had been mistreated by her family on so many levels. Now Lauren was called on to be the dutiful daughter—to come home to be at her mother's bedside in her final days. Lauren felt mixed emotions about returning home. She wanted to care for her dying mother, but their relationship was full of immense unresolved pain.

Vengeance would mean having the last word by refusing to go. But today's passage changed Lauren's heart, and she felt the Lord guiding her in a different direction. The Lord commands us to leave vengeance to him; he will repay with justice we can trust. Instead, we are encouraged to "heap burning coals" on our enemies' heads by doing good to them. Doing good to our enemies may cause them to feel ashamed of their behavior and possibly lead them to repentance. Even if the enemy does not repent, we can rest, knowing that our wrongdoer will face the Judge and just punishment on the last day. That knowledge can free our hearts to "not be overcome by evil, but overcome evil with good." Instead of giving in to the sins of judgment and vengeance against another, we can trust God's perfect justice and use our energy to be good to all.

Lauren returned home for the final month of her mother's life. She released vengeance to God. She did good to her mother, literally feeding her and giving her water to drink. She advocated for her in hospice, read God's Word to her, and sang hymns of grace. Unexpectedly, Lauren's goodness inspired her mother's heart to soften. She professed faith in Christ before her final day.

Our amazing God used Lauren's good to overcome evil!

Sadly, other members of Lauren's family did not respond in the way her mother had. They continue to be hard-hearted and a source of immense pain. Christian love compels Lauren to pray for their repentance, and so she does. However, God's wisdom also gives her freedom to create practical boundaries in those relationships so that she is safe from their abuse. Romans 12:18 says, "If possible, so far as it depends on you, live peaceably with all." Sometimes, particularly in abusive relationships, it is *not* possible to live peaceably among one another, and creating rules of engagement becomes a necessity, not a sin.[1] Forgiveness does not require you to place yourself in an unsafe situation.

Lauren's example shows us the tangible fruit of loving your enemy. May we all grow in our ability to leave vengeance in the Lord's hands. It starts by taking our enemies to the Lord in prayer and getting our hearts right by the power of his Spirit. Let us not be overcome by evil but overcome evil with good.

Reflect: Who are you tempted to avenge yourself against? How do you find yourself exacting vengeance?

Reflect: Do you repay evil for evil in quiet, subtle ways or in a loud, more conspicuous manner?

Act: Confess your temptation to repay evil for evil. Tell God and trusted friends. Pray for help to leave vengeance to God, and ask others to pray for you about this as well.

Act: If you have experienced abuse of any kind, talk to a wise counselor about how best to respond in your unique situation.

DAY 25

Cry Out to God

Humble yourselves, therefore, under the mighty hand of God so that at the proper time he may exalt you, casting all your anxieties on him, because he cares for you. (1 Peter 5:6–7)

WE HAVE SPENT several days considering how to forgive. Forgiveness is much harder than reading words on a page, isn't it? When we set out to forgive, we may feel as if we take one step forward and two steps back. We genuinely choose to forgive but are surprised at how much pain we still feel and how often the memories come back to haunt us. We become exhausted by rebuilding a relationship that has become messy with sin, even if that sin is forgiven.

After you forgive, life can still feel challenging. The person you forgave can continue to disappoint you, or you might even disappoint yourself with bitterness that won't go away. If this is you, may the apostle Peter encourage you today. "Humble yourselves, therefore, under the mighty hand of God so that at the proper time he may exalt you, casting all your anxieties on him, because he cares for you."

I wonder what you think of when you imagine "the mighty hand of God." For me, images of God's many famous rescues in Scripture fill my mind: God's mighty hand parting the Red Sea so the slaves could go free. God's mighty hand securing Daniel's safety in the lions' den. His mighty hand winning David's victory over Goliath. His mighty hand casting out demons, healing diseases, and giving sight to the blind in the New Testament. God's awesome, mighty hand defeating Satan, sin, and death once and for all on the cross of Christ. This is the mighty hand that Peter entreats you to humble yourself under today.

To humble yourself under the mighty hand of God means to remember who you are in light of who God is. You are frail; he is powerful. You are fallen; he is perfect. Put away your pride, and bring your weary, needy heart to God. Trust God's plans and God's timing in your life. He will exalt you at the proper time and in the proper way, according to his good purposes.

And remember, God is not only mighty. He *cares*. Peter reminds us of this as one who knew God's care personally. This was the disciple who tried to walk on water with Jesus but got scared and fell in. When he humbly cried out, "Lord, save me" (Matt. 14:30), what did Jesus do? "Jesus immediately reached out his hand and took hold of him, saying to him, 'O you of little faith, why did you doubt?'" (Matt. 14:31).

Forgiving is a little like walking on water. It requires faith to choose to forgive in God's strength. It takes humility to trust God when you're sinking into bitterness. Cry out to God with all of your anxiety. He cares for you, and he will lift you up.

Reflect: Do you feel weary or frustrated or hopeless in your forgiveness process right now? In what way might you need to humble yourself before the Lord?

Act: Write down a list of your anxieties. Look at the list and imagine whether God's mighty hand from Scripture is big enough for the items on your list. Like Peter, cry out for help, remembering that your God cares for you.

GOD HELPS US
TO FORGIVE

*"We talk glibly about forgiving when we have
never been injured; when we are injured we know
that it is not possible, apart from God's grace,
for one human being to forgive another."*

Oswald Chambers, *The Place of Help*

DAY 26

God's Spirit Strengthens You

I bow my knees before the Father, from whom every family . . . is
named, that according to the riches of his glory he may grant you to
be strengthened with power through his Spirit in your inner being,
so that Christ may dwell in your hearts through faith—that
you . . . may . . . know the love of Christ that surpasses knowledge,
that you may be filled with all the fullness of God. (Eph. 3:14–19)

SANCTIFICATION IS NOT an overnight process. We know
this, yet it is discouraging when we wish to change, only to keep
sinning in the same ways. In the place of forgiveness, we find more
of the same anger, bitterness, fear, and pride. Rebuilding relationships in the wake of sin is a messy process.

In our passage today, we draw from one of the most encour-
aging prayers of Scripture: the apostle Paul's prayer on behalf of
the Ephesian Christians. He prays to God the Father, who is sovereign over every family in heaven and earth, rich in glory. Paul
prays for the Ephesians to be strengthened with power through
God's Spirit in their inner being. He asks that Christ would dwell
in their hearts through faith. He prays the Ephesians could fully
fathom the love of Christ and be filled with the fullness of God.

That prayer really encourages me. It reminds me that we're
not left to ourselves in the process of change! God grants us *power* through his Spirit. The same Holy Spirit that takes residence
inside our hearts when we become Christians also strengthens
us with power in our inner being as we *grow* as Christians. We
can ask for God's power, and he will supply it in our inner being!
Christ dwells in our hearts through faith.

Forgiveness is hard. Even as I wrote this devotional, I found
myself struggling to forgive as God forgives. My husband, my

parents, my friend, even a stranger on the bus who yelled at me
. . . God provided me with numerous examples to keep it fresh
in my mind just how difficult forgiveness really is. Let's not lose
heart as we fall short of godliness in this area. God "is able to do
far more abundantly than all that we ask or think, according to the
power at work within us" (Eph. 3:20). No matter what your faith
struggle, or sin struggle, happens to be today, God has good news
for you. God's *Spirit* is at work in your inner being, and *Christ*
dwells in your heart through faith! Hallelujah!

Each time we struggle with forgiveness, let us bow our knees
before the Father. Ask God for his power through his Spirit. Ask
him to fill you with his fullness. Believe God's Word when it says
that he can do far more than we even imagine or think.

Reflect: You cannot forgive with your own weak striving. Are
you willing to ask the Father for *his* power? Paul Miller writes,
"Self-will and prayer are both ways of getting things done. At
the center of self-will is me, carving a world in my image, but
at the center of prayer is God, carving me in his Son's image."[1]
How is your prayer life? Do you believe that prayer is one of
God's primary instruments of change in your life?

Act: Use Scripture to fuel your prayer life. Pray the words of
Ephesians 3:14–19, and apply them to your desire to forgive.

DAY 27

Jesus Sympathizes with You

For we do not have a high priest who is unable to sympathize with our weaknesses, but one who in every respect has been tempted as we are, yet without sin. Let us then with confidence draw near to the throne of grace, that we may receive mercy and find grace to help in time of need. (Heb. 4:15–16)

FRIEND, AS YOU engage the difficult task of forgiving another person—and as you find yourself weak for that task—be encouraged that your great high priest sympathizes with your weaknesses.

Notice two things about Jesus, our great high priest, in today's passage.

First, *he can sympathize with our weakness.* Jesus was tempted in every way we are; he fully understands the hardship we endure. As Hebrews 12:3 says, "Consider him who endured from sinners such hostility against himself, so that you may not grow weary or fainthearted." Jesus sympathizes with your experience of betrayal and wrongdoing at the hands of another. He, better than anyone, knows the heartache and pains of your life. Draw near to your Great High Priest as you struggle. You can be confident that Jesus "gets it."

Second, *he was tempted in every respect as we are, yet without sin.* While Christ identifies with our weaknesses, having suffered and been tempted to a greater extent than we will ever be, he is unique in that he never sinned. Today, from his heavenly throne, our Lord Jesus Christ eagerly offers you the divine strength and perfection embodied in him. You are weak, but he is strong. He is approachable, and he is able.

Jesus not only understands, but he is also wholly sufficient to come to your aid. Today's passage assures us that Christ

73

sympathizes with our weaknesses, *and* he can supply mercy and grace to us when we need it most. You see, there is mercy and grace waiting for you in your time of need. Turn to Christ for the mercy and grace that you cannot find within yourself.

Jesus "was despised and rejected by men, a man of sorrows and acquainted with grief" (Isa. 53:3). He most certainly can relate to you. It can be difficult to share personal struggles with a friend or family member who doesn't fully understand. Jesus *fully understands*. What's more, he can help you in your time of need.

In verse 16, the author of Hebrews turns to you and says, "Let us then with confidence draw near to the throne of grace." Now that we know who Jesus is, we can—because of Jesus—approach God's throne for help.

You have the extraordinary privilege of a personal relationship with God himself. Friend, *draw near* to God's throne of grace with confidence.

Reflect: Which of your weaknesses come to mind as you read today's passage? Do you believe Jesus sympathizes with you? What would it look like for you to draw near to the throne of grace?

Act: Boldly approach the Lord in prayer, and speak to him plainly and honestly. Relate with the God whom you have a relationship with! He will hear you and help you.

DAY 28

God's Comfort Blesses You

Blessed be . . . the Father of mercies and God of all comfort, who comforts us in all our affliction, so that we may be able to comfort those who are in any affliction, with the comfort with which we ourselves are comforted by God. For as we share abundantly in Christ's sufferings, so through Christ we share abundantly in comfort too. (2 Cor. 1:3–5)

AS I MEET with men and women who have suffered greatly, I hear a similar sentiment over and over again: they would never want to relive their pain, but they would never remove their pain from their stories, because through their suffering they experienced more of God. Tell this to someone who is new to affliction or doesn't know God yet, and they will look at you quizzically. But many Christians will attest that suffering was the conduit to their knowing God more fully. Our testimony of knowing God can be so intricately woven together with our experience of affliction that we could not wish it had never happened. When we suffered, God ministered to us in the darkness. *Blessed be the God and Father of our Lord Jesus Christ, who comforts us in all our affliction.* The Lord comforts us. He loves us. He carries us. He shows us more of himself. As God comforts us in our sufferings, he brings us closer to himself.

Suffering drives us to the end of ourselves, and the Father of mercies uses that self-insufficiency to lead us to him, the God of all comfort.

Opponents of the apostle Paul pointed to *his* sufferings to argue that he was disqualified as an apostle. But Paul knew better. His sufferings were the means God used to strengthen the believers around him. He could bless God as a Father of mercies and God of all comfort because he had *personally* experienced God's sufficient strength in his times of trouble (see 2 Cor. 12:1–10), and he drew on God's comfort to comfort suffering Christians around him.

Christ himself suffered greatly, and we as believers will share in those sufferings, but we also share in the comfort of God through Christ. If you are in the midst of affliction right now, these words may not yet encourage you, but I pray they will soon. My pastor has said, "Waiting is what we do on a God whose purposes take place over time."[1] Wait on the Lord. Pray for his Spirit, for his comfort. He will not let you down, even if his faithfulness is revealed over time.

As you do the hard work of forgiving people who have hurt you, God will meet you in that difficult process. Someone caused you pain—maybe that person continues to cause you pain. Your suffering from that pain is *not* the end of the story. God's comfort is. The Lord will give you more of himself. Do not run from the work of forgiveness; instead, lean into God's comfort as you suffer. He will help you through it, that you might be able to comfort others with the comfort you receive.

Reflect: Have you experienced God's comfort in the midst of your suffering? Are you seeking his comfort? Is it possible that he is offering comfort in ways you're missing?

Act: Seek out a mature Christian you know who has suffered and persevered in their faith. Ask that person how they experienced the Lord's comfort in their suffering.

DAY 29

Jesus Offers You Rest

"Come to me, all who labor and are heavy laden, and I will give you rest. Take my yoke upon you, and learn from me, for I am gentle and lowly in heart, and you will find rest for your souls. For my yoke is easy, and my burden is light." (Matt. 11:28–30)

JESUS INVITES US to come to him for rest.

Christ spoke today's verses to a crowd crushed by the weight of trying to earn their salvation through good works. This foolishness was taught to them by the religious leaders of their day. But our Lord invited them into something unequivocally different from a law of righteousness by works. He asked them to trust in him *personally* for their salvation. "Come to me . . . and I will give you rest," he said.

Jesus told the people to take his "yoke" upon them. Consider that word picture of a yoke. In Jesus's day, it was a wooden frame that joined two oxen together to pull a heavy load. A yoke required the subjection of one to another in order to share a great burden. Jesus told the crowds that they could take *his* yoke on them! He promised that his yoke was easy and he could lighten their load. Jesus described himself as gentle and lowly, one who could give them rest for their souls. Ultimately, that rest is found through simple faith and commitment to him—so simple it seems that children understand best what Christ was getting at (see Matt. 11:25–26).

Jesus invites *you* to find rest in him for *your* soul. No matter what burdens you bear, he can help you. He beckons you: "Come to me, all who are weary and burdened." Do you feel weary today? Will you turn to him? Paul Miller writes, "The criteria for coming to Jesus is weariness. Come overwhelmed with life. Come with your wandering mind. Come messy."[1] This fits with Jesus's words in our passage today, doesn't it?

Jesus doesn't say, "Come to me when you get yourself together."

He doesn't say, "Come to me when you are emotionally mature and more reasonable and less sinful."

He doesn't say, "Come to me when you get better at forgiveness."

Jesus says, "Come to me, *all you who are weary and burdened*, and I will give you rest."

Go to Jesus today. Don't wait. Put your trust in him. We are sinners in need of a savior, and *he* is that Savior! Taking on his yoke releases you from the burden of saving yourself. His yoke also releases you from lifting the heavy load of forgiveness. So, weary saint, come to him now. Jesus bids you, "Come to me."

Engage with Jesus in a personal way. Read his Word. Trust his Word. Pray to him from the core of your being. Don't hold back. He is gentle and humble. He can give you rest. Don't let anything get in the way of running to him today.

Reflect: What barriers keep you from spending time with Jesus? Busyness? Pride? Shame? Laziness? What priorities make it to your daily routines when prayer does not?

Act: If you're having trouble fitting time with the Lord into your daily routine, start small. Commit to reading God's Word for five minutes a day and praying a prayer connected to what you read. See how God might minister to you even from that small change to your daily routine.

DAY 30

God's Power Is Sufficient for You

I will boast all the more gladly of my weaknesses, so that the power of
Christ may rest upon me. For the sake of Christ, then, I am content
with weaknesses, insults, hardships, persecutions, and calamities.
For when I am weak, then I am strong. (2 Cor. 12:9–10)

FORGIVENESS IS BIGGER than we are. We are weak for the
task of forgiveness. The good news is that when we are weak, God
is strong.

The apostle Paul was well-acquainted with weakness. As
we know from 2 Corinthians 12:1–10, he experienced a trial
that, whatever it may have been, tormented him a great deal. He
begged God to remove the tormenting trial, but God answered
those prayers differently than Paul had hoped. Instead of remov-
ing the trial, God told Paul that his grace and power would be
sufficient for him in his time of weakness. Astonishingly, Paul ex-
claims that he will *boast* all the more gladly of his weaknesses!
Why? So that the power of Christ could rest upon him. Paul became *content* with weakness, hardship, and calamities, because
difficulties drove Paul to God for strength. "For when I am weak,"
says Paul, "then I am strong." God's strength is made perfect in
weakness. Hallelujah!

God's grace is utterly sufficient for all our darkest moments
and deepest struggles. When we are weak, God's strength becomes evident as we rely on him.

I saw God's sufficient grace in Angela's life. She was a new
mom of a small baby, and her young husband had died of cancer.
There was so much to grapple with—the shock of motherhood,
loss of her life partner, lack of sleep, reduced finances, and a baby
to be raised without his father. Going into my first appointment

with her, I felt concerned that this might be the hardest counseling I'd ever do.

However, to my surprise, Angela spoke with unusual courage and ministered to me more than I ministered to her! She was open about her sadness, fear, and even anger at losing her husband, but she also expressed palpable faith. When she spoke of her frustrations about raising her son alone, for instance, she said, "The same God who was faithful to bring my husband to heaven is the same God who will sustain me in parenting. This is not the life I would have chosen for myself, but I can trust him." God had not answered Angela's prayers the way she had expected or hoped, yet it was very clear that he was upholding her faith and hope with his sufficient strength.

In our weakness, we discover God's strength. Weakness enables us—indeed, forces us—to release our petty notions of self-reliance. We are left with no option but to lean into God's infinite power. And that is the greatest gift—to know God's grace as fully sufficient, no matter the circumstance. His grace is peace in the eye of the storm.

God's grace is sufficient for you when you are bewildered by someone else's sin. It is sufficient when you feel weak at forgiving. No matter your circumstances, God will give you grace in your moments of need. His power can be made perfect in your weakness. Trust him.

Reflect: Has God ever shown you unexpected strength in a time when you really needed it? Do you believe that experiencing his grace to persevere through your trial may be better than even having him remove the trial altogether?

Act: When you feel weak because of your sin, or the sins of someone else, read 2 Corinthians 12 out loud and pray for God to show you his sufficient grace.

DAY 31

Christ's Victory Secures You

Behold, the dwelling place of God is with man. He will dwell with
them, and they will be his people, and God himself will be with them
as their God. He will wipe every tear from their eyes, and death shall
be no more, neither shall there be mourning, nor crying, nor pain
anymore, for the former things have passed away. (Rev. 21:3–4)

ONE DAY GOD will bring us to his dwelling place. There we
will experience the peace and joy of unhindered fellowship with
our Creator, the Lover of our souls. We will be completely reconciled, utterly reunited. He will be our God, dwelling with us, and
we will know full acceptance as his people. In heaven there will
be no more crying, no more mourning, no more pain at all. Our
sin will have passed away and so will the sins of others against us.

With your mind fixed on the reality of your final destination,
can you feel a renewed sense of strength that might enable you to
forgive what seems too painful to forgive? Why?

If Christ's victory on the cross secures for us the greatest of all
gifts—justification and reconciliation with God—then we know
the end of the story. We will be with God for all eternity. Our future is secure in Christ! That victorious end to our story makes a
difference in how we live *right now*. If we know this glorious, pain-
less future awaits us, doesn't that make it possible to forgive and
to give to others on our way to that heavenly home?

My son loves superhero books and movies. He is kind of
young still, so when a bad guy enters the story I will often ask,
"James, are you scared?" He always tells me no. Recently I asked
him why he never gets scared of the bad guys, and he matter-of-
factly told me, "Because they never win!" James knows the ending to any good superhero narrative. His favorite characters will

celebrate victory, and it will be a happy ending. So why fret on the way there?

Similarly, knowing the end of *our* story changes the way we perceive our current circumstances. When we experience difficult relational pain, we look to the day when we will have joyous unhindered fellowship with God and his people. On that day, and on the days that follow it into infinity, we will not hurt, or cry, or mourn ever again. We will never again feel the effects of our own or other people's sins. We will not harbor resentment or anger because we will be too overwhelmed by the glory of God.

As we fix our eyes on heaven, the relational wrongs of others begin to pale. May God refresh our strength to forgive, as we anticipate the glory that awaits us in our heavenly home.

Reflect: Does the thought of heaven astound you or leave you feeling ho-hum? How can the promises of heaven encourage you today?

Act: This life is a breath compared with the eternal hope of heaven, so let that propel you to boldness in forgiving others. Read more about heaven in Revelation 21 and 22. Soak in the promises of the life to come.

Conclusion

WHEN I DECIDED to write on forgiveness, I imagined I was "good" at forgiveness! The minute I actually set out to write about forgiveness, however, the Lord graciously revealed to me just how difficult forgiveness continues to be in my own life.

That's the trouble with forgiveness; it's not something you master once and move on. Life in a fallen world presents you with *unending* opportunities to forgive. Old conflicts recur in long-term relationships, and fresh conflicts crop up in new ones. Unresolved hurt feelings from old wounds will seep out and surprise us, and forgiveness will be the only antidote. We will find ourselves wrestling with forgiveness again and again.

This side of glory, we'll never stop needing to forgive. I expressed my surprise about this to an older saint. "Of course!" she chuckled. "We aren't going to stop forgiving till Jesus takes us home!" I love that about older saints. They aren't as rattled by the disturbing things that shock us younger Christians.

A Marathon, Not a Sprint

Forgiveness is a marathon, not a sprint. Back in my heyday, I was a long-distance runner, so I can tell you the difference between a marathon and a sprint. In a sprint, you go all-out. You expend every ounce of your strength to beat your opponent; there is no holding back. The race is over quickly, and the fastest runner wins, plain and simple. But in a long-distance race, endurance wins the race. You win a long-distance race not because you are the quickest, strongest, or most talented. You win a long-distance race because you *endure.*

To endure means to remain steadfast in the face of adversity. You persevere, even when the goal is hard. The road is long. The body is weak. That's when you endure. The good news about endurance is that, ultimately, it is an acquired skill. While speed, strength, and talent can be innate for some, endurance is grown over time, with hard work and a will to try.

Friend, *forgiveness is a race of spiritual endurance.* If long-distance running isn't your sport, be encouraged! You don't run the race of forgiveness alone. When you set out to endure in forgiveness over the long haul of your life, it is Jesus Christ, the founder and perfecter of your faith, who equips you for the battle.

As the author of Hebrews so wonderfully puts it, "Since we are surrounded by so great a cloud of witnesses, let us also lay aside every weight, and sin which clings so closely, and let us run with endurance the race that is set before us, looking to Jesus, the founder and perfecter of our faith, who for the joy that was set before him endured the cross, despising the shame, and is seated at the right hand of the throne of God" (Heb. 12:1–2).

Following the examples of the faithful saints of old, let's lay aside every burden of our sinful hearts to run the race of forgiveness—ultimately a race of faith. We train by turning away from sin and turning to the gospel each time we are tempted to withhold forgiveness from others. We cast aside the weights of anger, bitterness, judgment, and wrath and look to Jesus for the strength to endure the struggle of it all. He founded our faith, and he can and will protect our faith. We endure a hard road now, but he endured the even harder road to the cross. We can trust him for everything we need in order to endure.

If there's one thing I learned from my high school cross-country coach, it was to never look at the finish line but to look beyond it. She told us if we looked at the finish line, we would inevitably slow down on our way to it. But if we looked *beyond* the finish line, we would run full speed all the way *through* it. As we persevere in this life, let us look beyond the finish line to Jesus himself.

He is where we are going. He has already won the race for us! Now, with the help of his Spirit, we can run in faith and forgiveness all the way until he calls us home.

Where Do You Go from Here?

You have completed this devotional, yet there are many more miles to run before you reach the finish line. You'll need Christ's help to continue growing in forgiveness. Let me offer you next steps—seven suggestions as we wrap up.

1. Consider rereading this book. A second time through may help you to own the material more. The first time you read it, you were getting familiar with the content. The second time, you can internalize the lessons more. At the very least, look back at the days that you found particularly useful.

2. If there were Scripture texts that the Spirit used to encourage you, memorize them and make them your own. Tell friends about them. Write them down on a note card and carry them with you. Stick them up by the mirror. Pray through them often.

3. Meditate on Matthew 18:21–35 for thirty-one days in a row. Focus especially on verses 23–27. Soak the passage in. Apply it to your life. Talk about it with wise friends. Pray through it often. See if doing so softens your heart.

4. Read a recommended book or booklet on the resources list at the end of this book. All these resources will encourage you to continue your growth in gospel-centered forgiveness.

5. If you are not part of a local, Bible-believing, Jesus-loving church, then find one and join it quickly. Sitting under the preaching of the Word weekly is vital for your soul. Rubbing shoulders with genuine believers will help you to fight for a forgiving heart—not just for thirty-one days but for a lifetime.

6. If you're still struggling to forgive, consider finding a biblical counselor to get more help. A thoughtful, caring, and competent counselor can make a world of difference.

7. Be sure you are reading God's Word and praying. A month-long devotional is helpful, but it is no substitute for a personal relationship with Christ.

Acknowledgments

THIS DEVOTIONAL WOULD not exist without the enthusiastic support of my dear husband, Rob. Thank you for your much-needed help—brainstorming ideas, revising my work, and corralling our kids while I tried to write. When it comes to the topic of forgiveness, you are truly better at it than anyone. I love you, and I'm grateful for you.

Thank you also to the man who wears many, *many* hats in my life: Deepak Reju. You are my counselor, teacher, supervisor, mentor, friend, brother, and now we can add *editor* to the list! Who knows where I'd be now without your prayerful guidance through the years. "Thank you" does not suffice.

Elizabeth Christiansen, thank you for your servant-hearted, wonderful help with my beloved Hannah Sue, Lydia, and James. They love you, and I sure love you too! And thanks to all my amazing friends and family who cheered me on to keep writing during a crazy season in my life as a mom. You never cease to spur me on "to love and good deeds" (Heb. 10:24)!

Thanks to Chesed Broggi, Emily Halle, and Liz Whyte for your helpful writing feedback, revisions and encouragements. Thank you to my community group and Moms in Prayer group who upheld me in prayer as I wrote. Thank you to the P&R Publishing staff for coordinating this series and allowing me to contribute and to Rush Witt and Amanda Martin in particular for offering wise suggestions all along the way.

APPENDIX

Frequently Asked Questions about Forgiveness

As a counselor, I have seen the following questions come up frequently for people working through forgiveness. My answers are brief, so please check out the excellent books in my resources page for further study.

Does Forgiving Mean Condoning or Excusing Hurtful Behaviors?

Forgiveness should not minimize pain caused by another person. On the contrary, forgiveness stares real pain in the face, honestly, and prayerfully chooses to forgive it with God's help. Forgiveness does not mean avoiding confrontation of sin either. Sometimes it is appropriate to overlook an offense (see Prov. 19:11; Day 20), but other times it may be necessary to confront the sin in a biblical manner (see Matt. 18:15–17; Day 21).

Should I Forgive and Forget?

Forgetting is not something you can control, so it's an unrealistic expectation. However, to forgive does mean that you do not intentionally dwell on the wrongs of others. Brooding over the sins committed against you will only lead to discouragement and resentment. Even when you have genuinely decided to forgive someone, painful memories may flood back in from time to time. Let such moments become opportunities to return to God for help with forgiving. Fight the temptation to dwell upon the painful memory, and instead set your mind upon things that are above (see Phil. 4:8–9; Day 15).

Is Forgiveness the Same
as Reconciliation?

Think of forgiveness as having both a vertical and horizontal dimension. The vast majority of Scripture speaks to the vertical dimension of forgiveness—that is, one's heart attitude of forgiveness before the Lord (see Mark 11:25; Day 16). God commands us to unilaterally, unconditionally forgive others in our hearts every time we are sinned against. The Bible also speaks of a horizontal transaction of forgiveness that occurs between us and our offenders (see Luke 17:3; Days 10, 21). Another word for this is *reconciliation*. When a relationship is broken because of sin, both parties should try to seek reconciliation. Depending on the situation, however, reconciliation may or may not be fully possible. An offender's unrepentant sin, for example, may make reconciliation too difficult, or even unsafe. The heart attitude of forgiveness before God is always required, even when relational reconciliation is not possible or is unwise.

Am I Supposed to Forgive Someone Who Has
Not Admitted Fault or Shown Repentance?

When a wrongdoer refuses to admit fault or repent, you may not be able to fully reconcile relationally with that person (see Matt. 18:15–17; Day 23). Even so, God calls you to pursue a heart attitude of full forgiveness of that person (see Matt. 6:14–15; Day 23). Just as God has forgiven you, so you must also forgive.

Is Forgiveness a One-Time
Occurrence or a Process?

It is both. As we strive to become more like Christ in every way, we make a decision to follow his example at a certain moment in time, but in our human frailty we struggle with the follow-through process. We are all in need of continued help from

God's Spirit to grow and change. Do not lose heart when you set out to forgive and find it to be difficult. Lean into God's sufficient grace each time you are reminded of your human limitations (see 2 Cor. 12:9; Days 26, 30).

Notes

Introduction
1. Donna Terrell, "Donna Terrell's Special Report: Mother Forgives Son's Killer," Fox16.com, July 10, 2015, http://www.fox16.com /crime/donna-terrells-special-report-mother-forgives-sons-killer /210680526.
2. If you have been physically, emotionally, spiritually, or sexually abused, the conversation about forgiveness gets much more complicated. Talk to a pastor or counselor to sort through how best to respond to abuse, specific to your unique situation. I will say this one thing though—forgiveness does not mean that you should submit to abuse. Get help to get safe, now.

Day 3: Trust God's Free Gift of Grace
1. Julia H. Johnston, "Marvelous Grace of Our Loving Lord," 1911.

Day 8: Forgiveness Is Unfair
1. David Powlison, *Good and Angry: Redeeming Anger, Irritation, Complaining, and Bitterness* (Greensboro, NC: New Growth Press, 2016), 80.

Day 11: Forgiveness Is Debt-Canceling
1. Thomas Watson, *The Doctrine of Repentance* (CreateSpace Independent Publishing Platform, 2018). Originally published in 1668.

Day 23: Love Your Enemy
1. If you belong to a church that practices healthy church discipline, it might be possible for you to appeal to the church for further help in confronting your wrongdoer (see Matt. 18:15–17). Even if your wrongdoer is not a fellow church member, appealing to other people to come alongside you in confronting them may be helpful. Finding a biblical counselor to speak into your situation can also be helpful if reconciliation is not going smoothly.

2. To love and forgive your enemy is not the same as trusting them. Trust is good faith *earned* by the sustained integrity of another person, proven over time. While forgiveness is unconditional, trust is conditional upon the ongoing repentance of an offender.

Day 24: Leave Vengeance to the Lord

1. Sometimes you need to create boundaries in relationships that are abusive in nature. Consider this helpful advice from Christian writer and speaker Jen Wilkin: "The Bible takes great pains to address the dangers of keeping company with those who perpetually harm others. Those who learn nothing from their past mistakes are termed fools. While we may forgive the fool for hurting us, we do not give the fool unlimited opportunity to hurt us again. To do so would be to act foolishly ourselves. When Jesus extends mercy in the Gospels, he always does so with an implicit or explicit 'Go and sin no more.' When our offender persists in sinning against us, we are wise to put boundaries in place. Doing so is itself an act of mercy toward the offender. By limiting his opportunity to sin against us, we spare him further guilt before God. Mercy never requires submission to abuse, whether spiritual, verbal, emotional, or physical." *In His Image: 10 Ways God Calls Us to Reflect His Character* (Wheaton, IL: Crossway, 2018), 80–81.

Day 26: God's Spirit Strengthens You

1. Paul Miller, *A Praying Life: Connecting with God in a Distracting World* (Colorado Springs: NavPress, 2009), 160–61.

Day 28: God's Comfort Blesses You

1. Mark Dever, "The Lord's Love (Psalm 33:1–22)," Capitol Hill Baptist Church, September 18, 2016. Available at www .capitolhillbaptist.org/sermon/the-lords-love/.

Day 29: Jesus Offers You Rest

1. Paul Miller, *A Praying Life: Connecting with God in a Distracting World* (Colorado Springs: NavPress, 2009), 32.

Suggested Resources
for the Journey

DeMoss, Nancy Leigh. *Choosing Forgiveness: Your Journey to Freedom*. Chicago, IL: Moody Publishers, 2008. [This book is a sweet meditation on what the Bible says about forgiveness, as well as how forgiving others (or not forgiving them) can impact our lives. It is practical and accessible, with a warm, compassionate tone.]

Jones, Robert D. *Forgiveness: I Just Can't Forgive Myself*. Phillipsburg, NJ: P&R Publishing, 2000. [This short booklet addresses the difficulty of self-forgiveness that many Christians experience over sins from their past. Jones addresses wrong assumptions that accompany ongoing guilt and points the reader to the joyous gift of complete forgiveness in Christ.]

Lane, Tim. *Forgiving Others*. Greensboro, NC: New Growth Press, 2005. [In this short booklet of wise biblical counsel, Tim Lane asserts that we must know God's forgiveness in order to extend forgiveness to others, and he gives practical examples of how forgiveness can be shown in various situations.]

Lane, Tim, and Paul David Tripp. *Relationships: A Mess Worth Making*. Greensboro, NC: New Growth Press, 2006. [This book applies the gospel to relationships. In particular, I recommend chapter 9, "Forgiveness" (pp. 91–104). It offers helpful biblical insight about what forgiveness means, as well as how to practically show forgiveness in your relationships.]

Powlison, David. *Good and Angry: Redeeming Anger, Irritation, Complaining, and Bitterness*. Greensboro, NC: New Growth Press, 2016. [This book theologically and practically cuts to the heart of anger and bitterness (symptoms of unforgiveness). Chapters 7 and 8 (pp. 71–103) are especially relevant to the topic of forgiveness and could be read on their own. Chapter 7 is titled "The Constructive Displeasure of Mercy, Part 1: Patience and Forgiveness," and chapter 8 is titled "The Constructive Displeasure of Mercy, Part 2: Charity and Constructive Conflict."]

Sande, Ken. *The Peacemaker: A Biblical Guide to Resolving Personal Conflict*. Grand Rapids: Baker Books, 2004. [In this resource, Sande offers practical and biblical counsel for conflict resolution. I particularly recommend chapter 10, "Forgive as God Forgave You" (pp. 204–24), for helpful biblical guidance on the topic of forgiveness and how to apply it to your life.]

BIBLICAL
COUNSELING
COALITION

The Biblical Counseling Coalition (BCC) is passionate about enhancing and advancing biblical counseling globally. We accomplish this through broadcasting, connecting, and collaborating.

Broadcasting promotes gospel-centered biblical counseling ministries and resources to bring hope and healing to hurting people around the world. We promote biblical counseling in a number of ways: through our *15:14* podcast, website (biblicalcounselingcoalition.org), partner ministry, conference attendance, and personal relationships.

Connecting biblical counselors and biblical counseling ministries is a central component of the BCC. The BCC was founded by leaders in the biblical counseling movement who saw the need for and the power behind building a strong global network of biblical counselors. We introduce individuals and ministries to one another to establish gospel-centered relationships.

Collaboration is the natural outgrowth of our connecting efforts. We truly believe that biblical counselors and ministries can accomplish more by working together. The BCC Confessional Statement, which is a clear and comprehensive definition of biblical counseling, was created through the cooperative effort of over thirty leading biblical counselors. The BCC has also published a three-part series of multi-contributor works that bring theological wisdom and practical expertise to pastors, church leaders, counseling practitioners, and students. Each year we are able to facilitate the production of numerous resources, including books, articles, videos, audio resources, and a host of other helps for biblical counselors. Working together allows us to provide robust resources and develop best practices in biblical counseling so that we can hone the ministry of soul care in the church.

To learn more about the BCC, visit biblicalcounselingcoalition.org.

More from P&R Publishing

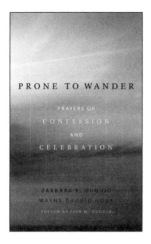
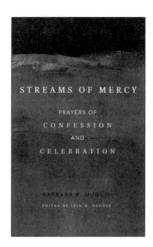

Confessing our sins might seem like a gloomy business . . . but exposing the specifics of our struggles with sin leads to celebration! It points us back to the good news of the gospel, our great Savior, and our forgiveness through God's grace.

Inspired by the Puritan classic *The Valley of Vision*, the prayers in these two volumes are ideal for use in church services or personal devotions. They open with a scriptural call of confession, confess specific sins, thank the Father for Jesus' perfect life and death in our place, ask for the help of the Spirit in pursuing holiness, and close with an assurance of pardon.

"[*Prone to Wander*] has many virtues. . . . The book covers the whole of the Christian life. I love its overall aims and method."
—Leland Ryken

"Here we learn how to pray God's Word back to him . . . and celebrate his grace in so many areas of our lives. I recommend [*Streams of Mercy*] strongly."
—John Frame

More Counseling Resources
from P&R Publishing

Bob Kellemen proves that we can have victory when anxiety strikes and even learn how to use it. In this biblical study, he lays out a proper Christian view of anxiety, from creation to fall to redemption to consummation. Along the way, he helps us to apply the gospel to our daily lives and reclaim anxiety for what it should be: *vigilance* to motivate us to do God's work.

Can the church truly help those who have been sexually abused? Bob Kellemen says yes, it can. He realistically portrays the damages wrought by sexual abuse and the relevancy of God's Word to this difficult topic. He then takes us on a journey toward healing, helping sufferers to reclaim beauty from the ashes of abuse and to move from being victims to victors.

The Gospel for Real Life booklet series by the Association of Biblical Counselors (ABC) applies the timeless hope of Christ to the unique struggles of modern believers.

Was this book helpful to you?
Consider writing a review online.
The author appreciates your feedback!

Or write to P&R at editorial@prpbooks.com
with your comments. We'd love to hear from you.